Essentials of ATM Networks and Services

Essentials of ATM Networks and Services

Oliver C. Ibe

ADDISON-WESLEY

An Imprint of Addison Wesley Longman, Inc.

Reading, Massachusetts • Harlow, England • Menlo Park, California
Berkeley, California • Don Mills, Ontario • Sydney
Bonn • Amsterdam • Tokyo • Mexico City

The publisher offers discounts on this book when ordered in quantity for special sales. For more information, please contact:

> Corporate & Professional Publishing Group
> Addison Wesley Longman, Inc.
> One Jacob Way
> Reading, Massachusetts 01867

Library of Congress Cataloging-in-Publication Data

Ibe. Oliver C. (Oliver Chukwudi)
    Essentials of ATM networks and services / Oliver C. Ibe.
        p.   cm.
    Includes bibliographical references and index.
    ISBN 0-201-18461-3
    1. Asynchronous transfer mode.   I. Title.
TK5105.35.I24 1997
  004.6'—dc21   97-17977
                                         CIP

2 3 4 5 6 7 MA 00 99 98 97

2nd Printing January, 1998

To Christie, Chidinma, Ogechi, Amanze, and Ugonna.

C O N T E N T S

PREFACE

The data communications and telecommunications industries are experiencing remarkable growth. One of the forces driving this growth is the **asynchronous transfer mode** (ATM) technology. Although ATM networks are not widely deployed at this time, they have already generated much curiosity and sparked much debate over how current and new telecommunications services will be offered. In short, ATM has the potential to change the nature of service provisioning in both the data communications and telecommunications industries.

This book is based in part on a series of lectures I gave as an introduction to ATM networks. The material came from several sources, including ATM Forum specifications, IETF RFCs and Internet-draft proposals, and ITU-T recommendations. As the title indicates, the book covers the essentials of ATM technology and summarizes the many services being defined over ATM networks. Any reader that is interested in more detailed information on any of the topics covered here should consult more advanced textbooks or the appropriate standards, recommendations, and specifications. I have tried to simplify the technical details with flow diagrams and examples. I hope that in the process I have maintained the delicate balance between technical correctness and simplicity of presentation.

As stated above, the focus of this book is on both ATM technology and the services that can be obtained from that technology. There is often the temptation to stress which of the emerging standards are relevant and which have been implemented. The problem with this line of thinking is that ATM standards are still evolving. A lot of time and resources have been spent by many people to develop these standards. To say that any one standard is not relevant is unfair to the people who have worked so hard on these standards to ensure that ATM succeeds. What has not been implemented today may be implemented tomorrow. For this reason, and in fairness to the many people who have worked so hard on the different standards committees, this book discusses many of the approved and evolving standards without considering their implementation. Moreover, since implementations are generally vendor specific, an attempt has been made to avoid discussing any implementation issues in order not to favor one vendor over others. In this respect, this book is different from other books on ATM.

It presents ATM technology and emerging and approved standards for the different services and leaves it up to the reader to judge what is relevant to him or her and what is not.

The first half of the book provides an overview of ATM technology. This includes Chapter 1 through Chapter 8. The second half, which starts at Chapter 9, attempts to explain the services that are being defined for ATM networks. These services include ATM LAN emulation, IP over ATM, multiprotocol over ATM, frame-based access services over ATM, audiovisual multimedia services over ATM, circuit emulation service, and inverse multiplexing over ATM. Most of these services are still being defined. However, it is my belief that the underlying architectures will not deviate radically from where they are today. Even if they do, the reader will gain enough understanding to follow the changes without being confused. Chapter 1 gives a comprehensive overview of telecommunication and networking basics. It also discusses the evolution of ATM networks, the major forces driving ATM networks, and the market for ATM networks. An extensive glossary of terms is provided at the end of the book.

This book is intended for data communications and information systems managers who want a quick reference on ATM networks. The book is also suitable for corporate courses on ATM networks and services. Because network experts tend to focus on one or two aspects of ATM technology, this book will be an appropriate resource for obtaining a quick overview of ATM networks. Finally, the book can also be used for an introductory graduate course in ATM networks.

Many networking technologies have been introduced since the advent of ATM. Some of them will impact ATM network services in one way or another. Two of these technologies are IP switching and the digital subscriber line family of technologies. The impact of IP switching on both the ATM Forum's multiprotocol over ATM and the IETF's IP over ATM is discussed briefly in Chapter 11. Similarly, the impact of the digital subscriber line family of technologies on ATM inverse multiplexing service is discussed in Chapter 15.

ACKNOWLEDGMENTS

I am grateful to Jianyu Zeng for the stimulating discussions we had on ATM. I am also grateful to Mark Ellis, Ravi Prakash, Matthew Scott, Ian Taylor, and Elizabeth (Betty) Zinkann for reviewing the manuscripts for the book and providing useful comments.

I would like to thank Mary Harrington of Addison Wesley Longman Publishing Company for her invaluable encouragement throughout the review process. I would also like to thank Melissa Lima, also of Addison Wesley Longman, for her hard work in ensuring the timely production of this book.

I am grateful to my employer, Xyplex Networks, for providing a very congenial work environment that made it possible for me to complete this book.

Finally, I am greatly indebted to my wife, Christina, and our children, Chidinma, Ogechi, Amanze, and Ugonna, for enduring my many hours away from them to write this book and for being my greatest fans. This book is dedicated to them. Christie and Chidinma also helped to proofread the final draft, and I am very grateful to them.

CHAPTER 1

Introduction

1.1 Telecommunications Primer

Communication is concerned with the distribution or exchange of information, knowledge, and ideas. A **message** is the information, knowledge, or idea that is being distributed or exchanged. Originally messages were only exchanged by people coming together to speak face to face. With the invention of writing, it became possible to carry messages from one place to another. This made possible communication-at-a-distance known as **telecommunication.** In its early stages, telecommunication was limited by how fast and how far the person carrying the message could go. The introduction of the telegraph and the telephone gave rise to electronic communication that removed the distance and time limitations on telecommunication [1].

Telecommunications usually refers to the technology of communication-at-a-distance. However, it means more than communication-at-a-distance. It is a **transporting** technology that transfers messages among information users, a **linking** technology that connects islands of information users, and an **enabling** technology that makes it possible for information that is created anywhere to be used anywhere in real time [1].

In the remainder of this chapter, the terms **message** and **data** are used interchangeably. Sending a message between two points requires three components:

1. The **source** generates the message.
2. The **transmission medium** (or **communication link**) is the connection over which the message is transported.
3. The **sink** (or **destination**) receives the message.

1

Several communication issues must be resolved before a message can be transferred from the source to the destination. These issues include the transmission method, the manner in which the source and destination are interconnected, the technique used to transfer the message, and the type of access control the source uses to launch the message in the network. The techniques used to resolve these issues are discussed in this section.

1.1.1 Transmission Method

When a message is transmitted by the source, some means must be provided for the destination to determine what information was transmitted. Two types of transmission methods are used: **asynchronous** transmission and **synchronous** transmission. Asynchronous transmission is used in applications where the message is generated as keyboard input. Asynchronous transmission is used to indicate that the data units are being transmitted as individual characters, each of which is preceded by one start bit and one or two stop bits. These start and stop bits are used by the receiver for synchronization purposes. The need for synchronization arises because the interval between characters may be random. As a result, the receiver may be idle for a long time after a character has been received. The start bit puts the receiver in a receiving mode and the stop bits return it to the idle mode.

Generally, asynchronous transmission is used when the interval between characters is indeterminate; the receiver may be idle for a long time between characters. Synchronous transmission is used in those applications, such as computer-to-computer transfers, where a preassembled large block of data needs to be transferred. In this case a complete block is transferred as a **frame**. Each frame is preceded by start bit and terminated by stop bits. Synchronous transmission is more efficient than asynchronous transmission because a set of start and stop bits is used for a block of more than one character, while the same set of bits is used for one character in asynchronous transmission. Also, it results in a higher transmission rate than asynchronous transmission.

1.1.2 Data Flow Direction

With respect to the direction of flow of data from the source to the destination, there are three methods that characterize a communication system: the **simplex** method, the **half duplex** method, and the **full duplex** method. In the simplex method, data can flow in one direction only, usually from the source to the destination. In the half duplex method, data can flow in both directions but not simultaneously. It first flows in one direction, and then in the other direction. In the full duplex method, data can flow in both directions simultaneously. A full duplex system may be viewed as a pair of simplex links between the source and the destination where data flows in one direction in one link and in the opposite direction in the other.

1.1.3 Network Topologies

A typical communication environment includes multiple sources and sinks. These devices, which are usually referred to as **nodes,** are connected by communication links in some manner to build a **network**. Network topology refers to the different configurations that can be used to build a network. These configurations include point-to-point, multidrop, bus, ring (or loop), star, tree, and mesh.

In a **point-to-point** topology, a link permanently connects two nodes. As we will see later, it is the basic building block for many of the other topologies. For example, Figure 1.1(a) shows two nodes, A and B, connected in a point-to-point manner and Figure 1.1(b) shows nodes C, D, E, F, and G connected in a **point-to-multipoint** manner. In the point-to-multipoint example, node C is connected to each of the other nodes in a point-to-point manner.

In the **multidrop** topology, a number of nodes, called **secondary nodes,** share one link that comes from the primary node. A multidrop link is also called a **multipoint** link. Figure 1.2 shows a multidrop topology in which node A is the primary node and nodes B–G are the secondary nodes.

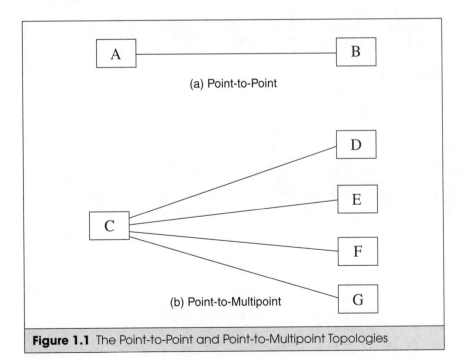

(a) Point-to-Point

(b) Point-to-Multipoint

Figure 1.1 The Point-to-Point and Point-to-Multipoint Topologies

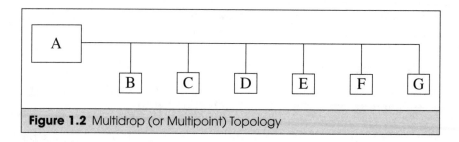

Figure 1.2 Multidrop (or Multipoint) Topology

In a **bus** topology, all the nodes are connected in a line to a single link, as in the multidrop topology. However, unlike the multidrop technology, there is no primary-secondary relationship; all nodes have a peer relationship. The link has two distinct ends, as Figure 1.3 illustrates. The Ethernet is an example of a network with the bus topology.

In a **ring** topology, the nodes are connected serially in a point-to-point manner with the last node connected to the first to form a loop. Figure 1.4 shows an example of a ring topology. A token ring network is an example of a network with the ring topology.

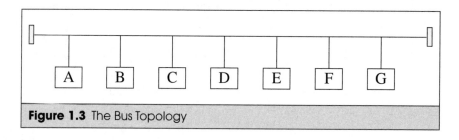

Figure 1.3 The Bus Topology

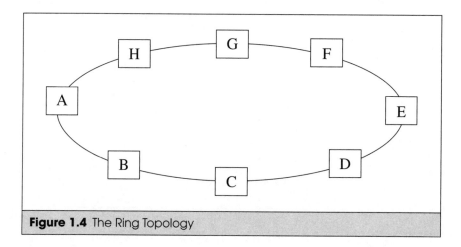

Figure 1.4 The Ring Topology

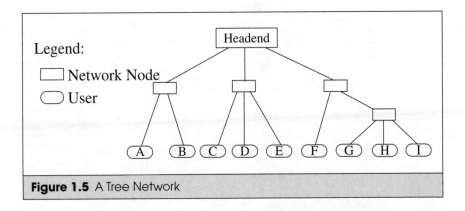

Figure 1.5 A Tree Network

The **star** topology is the same as the point-to-multipoint topology shown in Figure 1.1(b). Each node is connected in a point-to-point manner with a central node (or hub) that controls communication in the network. In Figure 1.1(b) node C is the hub.

The **tree** topology is a generalization of the bus topology. It is formed by connecting multiple buses together to form a system of branching links with no closed loops. Figure 1.5 shows an example of a network with the tree topology.

A tree topology usually has a special network node, called the **head-end**, from which information flows to all the end users. Two buses are connected by a node that acts to amplify the signal flowing from the headend to the users. The users form the leaves of the tree and the headend is the root of the tree. The cable television network is an example of a network with the tree topology.

In a **mesh** topology, communication is achieved by moving a message from the source to the destination through a set of nodes interconnected in an arbitrary manner. The function of these nodes is to provide a **switching** facility that moves the message from one node to another until it reaches its destination. Users are directly attached to only a subset of these nodes, as Figure 1.6 illustrates.

1.1.4 Geographical Coverage

Networks are sometimes classified by their geographical coverage. This gives rise to the local area network (LAN), the metropolitan area network (MAN), and the wide area network (WAN). A LAN is a high-speed network that spans a small geographical area, typically a floor or a set of floors in a building, an entire building, or a campus, and is owned by an organization. The Ethernet and the token ring network are local area networks. A MAN is a high-speed network designed to link together LANs in a campus or a metropolitan area. The fiber distributed data interface (FDDI) and the distributed queue dual bus (DQDB)

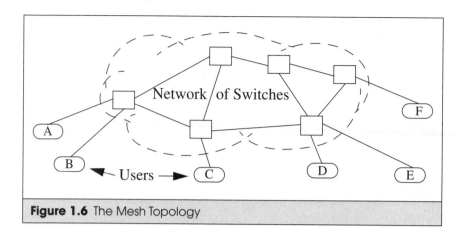

Figure 1.6 The Mesh Topology

are metropolitan area networks. A WAN is a network that covers a much larger area than a MAN, typically a region, state, or entire country. A WAN is usually a public network that is subject to some form of regulation. The telephone network is a wide area network.

1.1.5 Data Transfer Techniques

There are two ways in which data can be transferred from a source to a destination: **switching** and **broadcasting**. In a switched network, data is transferred from the source to the destination through a series of intermediate switching nodes. The data is moved from one node to another until it reaches its destination. There are two types of switching: **circuit switching** and **packet switching**.

In circuit switching, a dedicated communication path is established between the source and the destination which is used for the duration of their session. Circuit switching requires that the path first be established. Then the message is transferred and the path is torn down. The advantage of circuit switching is that once the path is established, messages are transferred continuously between the source and the destination with no delay other than the propagation delay; the delay at each node is negligible. However, the disadvantage of circuit switching is that it can lead to inefficient use of network resources if messages are not flowing continuously. In particular, if the duration of the session is short, the overhead incurred in setting up and tearing down the path may not be justified. Circuit switching is used in telephone networks.

Packet switching is an improved form of an older technique called **message switching**. In message switching, each message has a header that contains the addresses of the source and the destination and is sent into the network without setting up the path *a priori*. The message is transferred from the source to the destination in a **store-and-forward** manner. When the message arrives at a node, the node checks it for errors. If an error is found in the message, it is discarded. Otherwise, it is queued along with other messages; it will be forwarded to the next node on the path to its destination when it is its turn to be transmitted. The node uses a well-defined algorithm called a **routing algorithm** to determine the next node to receive the message. One major problem is that it gives rise to large delay variance because shorter messages tend to be queue behind longer messages and hence suffer long delays. As a result, message switching is not appropriate for real-time applications.

In packet switching, the message to be transferred is organized in units called **packets**. Each packet is then transferred from the source to the destination in a store-and-forward manner. Packet switching is used in data communication networks. There are two versions of packet switching: **datagram service** and **virtual circuit switching**. In datagram service, each packet in a multipacket message is routed independently at each node. As a result, packets may arrive out of order and may need to be resequenced at the destination. In virtual circuit switching, all the packets belonging to the same message follow the same path and arrive at the destination in the same order they were sent. Packet switching has the advantage that it leads to better network utilization than circuit switching since no resources are dedicated to any session.

A broadcast network is one in which no intermediate switching nodes are present. A transmission from one user is received by all users in the network. An example of a broadcast network is the local area network.

1.1.6 Network Access Techniques

There are two network access techniques that are closely tied to the types of data transfer techniques used. The two techniques are the **broadcast network access** and the **switched network access**. There are two types of broadcast network access: **random access** (or **contention**) and **polling** (or **controlled access**). Random access is generally used in a packet-switched network. In this scheme, two or more users share a common communication link and any user can commence packet transmission when the communication link is idle. If two or more users attempt to transmit on the link at the same time, their packets will "collide" and none of them will succeed in getting their packet to its destination. Generally a rule is available for resolving this conflict, ensuring that only one user transmits at a time. A variation of the random access scheme is used in the Ethernet.

In the polling system, transmission is done in a round-robin manner such that users take turns transmitting packets, thereby ensuring that no packet collision occurs. This is achieved in one of two ways: **centralized polling** or **distributed polling** (or **token passing**). In centralized polling, which is also called **roll call polling,** a control node determines the transmission order. It polls the users one by one, and a user can only transmit when it receives the poll signal. In the distributed polling scheme, there is no control node. Instead, a special packet called the **token** is passed from user to user. When a user receives the token, it takes the following action: If it has a packet for transmission, it will transmit its packet and then pass the token to the next user in a pre-defined polling order. If it has no packet to transmit, it passes the token to the next user. The process continues until a polling cycle is completed, wherein every user has had the opportunity to transmit and the process is repeated.

For a switched network there are two types of network access: **circuit-switched access** and **packet-switched access**. Circuit-switched access has three phases: the **call setup phase** during which a path is established between the source and the destination using a predefined procedure; the **data transfer phase** during which data is transmitted from the source to the destination and possibly from the destination to the source also; and the **call tear-down phase** during which the path between the source and the destination is torn down using a predefined procedure after all data has been transmitted. In packet-switched access, a user sends its packet into the network whenever the packet is ready. There is no call setup, as in the circuit-switched access, and the packet is routed in a store-and-forward manner as described earlier.

1.1.7 Multiplexing

In many applications, a communication link offers more transmission capacity than a single user can use. In this case the link can better be used through the process of **multiplexing**. Multiplexing allows more than one user to transmit information on a communication link. This can be done in either the frequency domain or in the time domain. When multiplexing is done in the frequency domain, we obtain **frequency-division multiplexing** (FDM). Similarly, when multiplexing is done in the time domain, we obtain **time-division multiplexing** (TDM).

In FDM, the total bandwidth (or the spectrum of frequencies that can be used for data transmission) is divided into independent **channels**. A user can transmit in one channel without affecting another user in another channel. All the channels generated in the link can be used simultaneously. FDM is used to partition the radio frequency spectrum, thereby making it possible for us to receive transmissions from different radio and television stations simultaneously. Figure 1.7 shows an FDM system with N channels.

In TDM, transmission time is divided into **time slots** of equal duration. Each user is assigned a time slot in which the user will transmit data. At the receiving end, the data stream from the different time slots is demultiplexed (or separated into different data streams) and each stream is delivered to the appropriate destination. Figure 1.8 shows a TDM system with slots for N users. The order of transmission is 1, 2, 3, ..., N, 1, 2, 3, ..., N, 1, ...

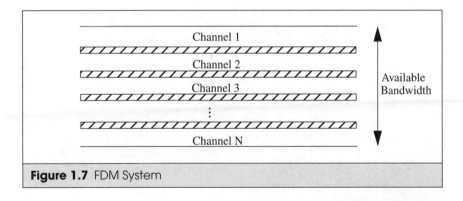

Figure 1.7 FDM System

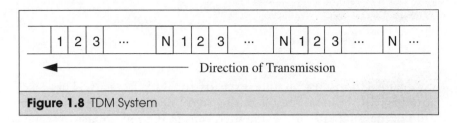

Figure 1.8 TDM System

The TDM described above is generally referred to as **synchronous TDM** since the time slots are assigned statically. Each time slot is dedicated to the user even when the user has nothing to transmit in a time slot. In a heavy traffic situation, where users usually have data to transmit in every slot, the link is efficiently utilized. However, in light traffic situations the link utilization is low since a large portion of the bandwidth is wasted. One way to handle this inefficiency is by using **statistical multiplexing** (or **asynchronous TDM**). Using this technique, which is used primarily in packet switching, no slot is dedicated to any user. Instead the **statistical multiplexer** (or **stat mux**) allocates slots dynamically only to active users (i.e., users that have packets to transmit). Specifically, as users' packets arrive at the multiplexer, they are sent into the slots in the same order that they are received by the multiplexer. Since each packet has a header that contains the address of the destination, the demultiplexer at the destination end separates the packets and delivers them to their appropriate users. Figure 1.9 shows a statistical multiplexing system serving six users, where some users are idle in their allocated time slot under the synchronous TDM scheme.

Figure 1.9 shows that as packets arrive, they are queued at the statistical multiplexer and transmitted on a first-come first-served basis.

The link efficiency can further be improved in statistical multiplexing by "overbooking" the link capacity. More calls can be admitted

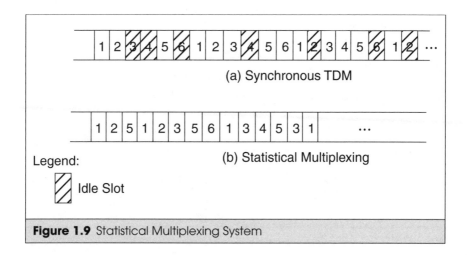

Figure 1.9 Statistical Multiplexing System

whose total transmission rate exceeds the link capacity. This takes advantage of the randomness in the on-off behavior of the users. The ratio of the total rate of the admitted calls to the link capacity is called **statistical multiplexing gain** (or **overbooking ratio**). For example, consider the system in Figure 1.10 where the value next to each link is the rate at which the user on that link may transmit. The aggregate data rate presented to the stat mux is 832 kbps. With the output of the stat mux at 256 kbps, the overbooking ratio is 768/256 = 3.0.

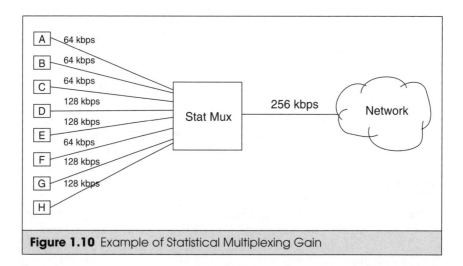

Figure 1.10 Example of Statistical Multiplexing Gain

1.2 Data Communication Network Architecture

Data communication is concerned with the exchange of data messages between data processing machines (computers). Transferring a message from one machine to another is not a trivial task. To simplify intermachine communication, the International Standards Organization (ISO) has proposed a seven-layer architectural model, called the Open Systems Interconnection (OSI) Reference Model [2], for implementing data communication between cooperating systems. The OSI model shows how to provide a wide range of communication services to computer systems from different vendors to achieve interoperability. Specifically, this architecture permits intercommunication among computer systems from different vendors. Each layer in the model deals with specific data communication functions.

The OSI model attempts to decompose the complexity of information flow between machines into a set of functions that are independent of each other. To achieve this independence, an upper layer is required to depend on services provided by the next lower layer. One advantage of this model is that the implementation of any layer can change with technology without affecting the implementation of the other layers as long as the services it provides the immediate upper layer remain the same.

Associated with each layer is a set of **layer entities** that perform functions defined by the **layer standard**. The layer standard consists of two parts: a **service definition,** which specifies the functions performed by the layer, and a **protocol specification,** which defines the procedures that are used to execute the layer functions. The entities in each layer exchange messages with peer entities in the other machine. Figure 1.11 shows the seven layers of the OSI reference model.

The functions performed in the layers are as follows:

- **Physical layer:** This is the lowest layer of the OSI model that defines the electrical and mechanical standards and signaling required to establish, maintain, and terminate connections. It deals with such things as the size and shape of connectors, electric signal strengths, bit representation, and bit synchronization. Typical physical layer protocols include the ITU-T X.21 [3] and the RS 232.

- **Data link layer:** This layer is responsible for preparing the data in a specific format (called a **frame**) for transfer over the link. It is responsible for detecting and correcting errors in a frame by requesting a retransmission. Typical data link layer protocols include the High Level Data Link Control (HDLC) [4], and the IBM Synchronous Data Link Control (SDLC) [5].

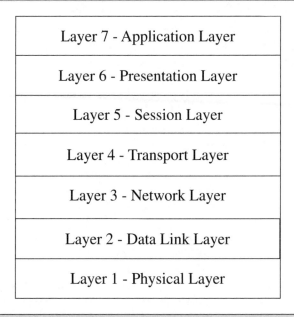

Figure 1.11 The OSI Reference Model

- **Network layer:** This layer is responsible for routing the data to its destination and for network addressing. A typical network layer protocol is the Internet Protocol (IP) [6].
- **Transport layer:** The transport layer is responsible for the reliable transfer of data between end systems regardless of the performance and number of networks involved in the connection between the communicating end systems. A typical transport layer protocol is the Transmission Control Protocol (TCP) [6].
- **Session layer:** The session layer is responsible for the establishment, maintenance, and termination of connections. It controls data transfer by structuring data exchange into a series of dialog units. This facilitates restarting the exchange if service is interrupted.
- **Presentation layer:** This layer is responsible for translating the information to be exchanged into terms that are understood by the end systems.
- **Application layer:** The application layer is responsible for providing end-user applications. Typical application layer protocols include the electronic messaging (X.400) protocol [7], and directory service (X.500) [8].

The lowest three layers (physical, data link, and network) perform networking functions. For communication that involves a source node, an intermediate node, and a destination node, all seven layers in the source and destination nodes, as well as the lowest three layers of the intermediate node, provide services to make the communication possible. Except for the lowest layer, the physical layer, each layer at the source end system adds header information called the **protocol control information** (PCI), which peer entities at the receiving node use to perform a service function. The data that layer N passes down to layer N-1 is called the N-1 **service data unit** (SDU). At layer N-1, the layer entities add the appropriate PCI to the SDU to generate the N-1 **protocol data unit** (PDU), which is then passed down to layer N-2. Figure 1.12 illustrates this process.

An entity in each layer provides service to the entities in the immediate higher layer through a **service access point** (SAP). The SAP through which a layer N entity provides service to a layer N + 1 entity is called a layer N + 1 SAP. The SAP through which a network layer entity provides service to a transport layer entity is called a **transport service**

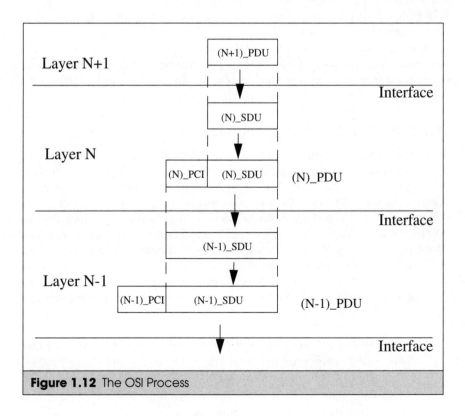

Figure 1.12 The OSI Process

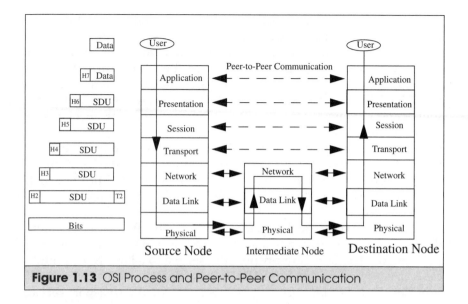

Figure 1.13 OSI Process and Peer-to-Peer Communication

access point (TSAP). Similarly, the SAP through which an entity in the data link layer provides service to a network layer entity is called a **network service access point** (NSAP).

Figure 1.13 illustrates the OSI process and the peer-to-peer communication that takes place in the communication between an end user on a source node and end user on a destination node with a network node (or switch) between the two nodes.

1.2.1 X.25 Network Architecture

ITU-T Recommendation X.25 defines the interface and access protocols between a data terminal equipment (DTE) and a packet switched data network [9]. Examples of DTE include a data terminal and a computer system. In an X.25 network, a data terminal equipment is connected to the packet switched data network via a data circuit-terminating equipment (DCE). The DCE controls the DTE's access to the packet-switched data network and X.25 is an interface specification that governs the interaction between the DTE and the DCE.

X.25 has a layered architecture with three levels corresponding to the lowest three layers of the OSI reference model. The three levels are as follows:

- The **Physical level** (or layer 1) is responsible for establishing physical connection between the DTE and DCE using one of three ITU-T recommendations: X.21, X.2 bis, or V.24.
- The **Data link level** (or layer 2) is equivalent to the OSI data link layer. It is also called the **frame level**. Its function is to provide a

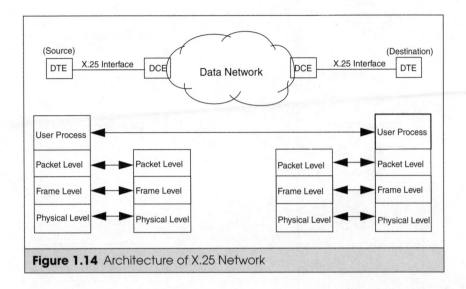

Figure 1.14 Architecture of X.25 Network

reliable transmission of data between the DTE and the DCE using the Link Access Protocol-Balanced (LAPB), which is a subset of the HDLC protocol.

- The **Packet level** (or layer 3) is at the network layer of the OSI reference model. It is responsible for setting up and tearing down virtual circuits, and for establishing the packet formats.

The X.25 network is a connection-oriented network that supports both the permanent virtual circuit and the switched virtual circuit. For a switched virtual circuit, the calling DTE establishes the circuit, transfers the data across the X.25 interface, and tears down the circuit. A permanent virtual circuit does not require a connection setup and tear down. Figure 1.14 illustrates the architecture of the X.25 network.

1.2.2 Internet Architecture

The Internet is the largest data network in the world. It is an interconnection of several packet-switched networks and has a layered architecture. Figure 1.15 shows the Internet layers and how they map into the OSI reference model.

The layers are as follows:

- **Network access layer:** No specific protocols are defined for this layer. It is expected that the network will rely on the data link and physical layer protocols of the appropriate networks. Thus, the network access layer is implementation-specific; protocols for local area networks, X.25, frame relay, and ATM may be used as appropriate.

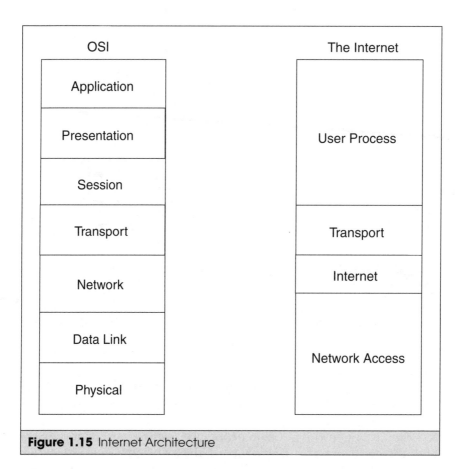

Figure 1.15 Internet Architecture

- **Internet layer:** This layer is the top part of the network layer. The Internet Protocol (IP) defined for this layer is a simple connectionless datagram protocol. It provides no error recovery; it performs error checking on each IP packet and discards any packet found to be in error without notifying the sender. IP supports data fragmentation that allows a protocol data unit to be segmented into two or more smaller units. It is an unreliable protocol because it does not guarantee that an IP datagram will be delivered to the destination.

  The internet layer defines an addressing scheme that permits both the network and the host machine receiving the packet in the network to be uniquely identified. There are four classes of IP addresses, A, B, C, and D, each of which uses 32-bit address. In the IP address for classes A, B, and C, the first portion defines the network ID and the second portion defines the ID of a host within the network. Class D addresses are reserved for multicast groups. An organization with a class A, B, or C IP address can subdivide the host ID portion of the IP address to provide subnetworks. Routing devices called **IP gateways** use the network ID portion of the IP address to route IP datagrams.

- **Transport layer:** Two protocols are defined for the transport layer: the Transmission Control Protocol (TCP) and the User Datagram Protocol (UDP).

  TCP is a connection-oriented protocol that permits the reliable transfer of data between the source and destination end users. It identifies protocol data units by sequence numbers that it uses to guarantee the delivery of the data it receives from user processes. It performs data flow control by sending a certain number of "credits" to the source host. This number, usually called the **window value,** is issued by the destination TCP and signifies the number of data octets the source host may send before an acknowledgment is returned to it. When this number of data octets has been sent, the source host will stop transmitting until it receives an acknowledgment that also includes the next window value. TCP does error checking on all received packets and delivers all error-free packets to the user process. If a packet is found to be in error, it is discarded together with all packets received after it in the current window. In this case the destination host returns an acknowledgment to the source host that indicates a window value which begins with the sequence number of the packet in error. The source host will then retransmit the packet with the error and any other packets that were transmitted after it. The source host must also transmit any new packets it has accumulated up to the value of the window.

  UDP is simpler than TCP and is designed for those applications that do not require the reliability and overhead of TCP. It is a connectionless protocol that offers neither error recovery and nor flow control. It checks each packet for errors. If no errors are found, it delivers the packet to the destination user process. A packet found to be in error is "silently discarded"; the packet is discarded with no further action taken. The TCP and UDP are usually referred to in combination with the IP as TCP/IP or UDP/IP.

- **User process layer:** This layer describes the applications and technologies that are used to provide end-user services. Application protocols that have been defined for this layer include the following:

  - **Simple Mail Transfer Protocol** (SMTP): This is a protocol that is used to exchange electronic mail between two hosts using TCP.
  - **Telnet:** This is a service that allows a user on a terminal to start a login session on a remote computer system. It uses TCP.

- **File Transfer Protocol** (FTP): This is a protocol that allows files to be sent from one computer system to another. It uses TCP and optionally provides user authentication using user ID and password.
- **Simple Network Management Protocol** (SNMP): This is a protocol that allows network devices, such as workstations, routers, and terminal servers, to be monitored and controlled from a network management station. It uses UDP.
- **Remote Procedure Call** (RPC): This is a protocol that is used in client-server systems. It allows a client process running on a local computer system to ask another process running on a remote system to perform some function. It uses UDP.
- **Trivial File Transfer Protocol** (TFTP): This is a simpler protocol than the FTP. It does not provide user authentication and uses the UDP.

Figure 1.16 shows the relationship of these user process protocols to the transport layer protocols. It contains only a partial listing of the Internet protocol stack.

1.2.3 SS7 Network Architecture

The concept of layered architecture has also been applied to the Signaling System Number 7 (SS7) [10], which defines procedures for call

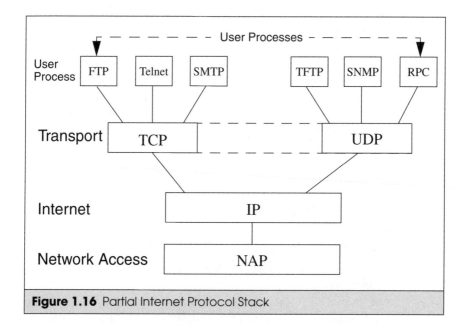

Figure 1.16 Partial Internet Protocol Stack

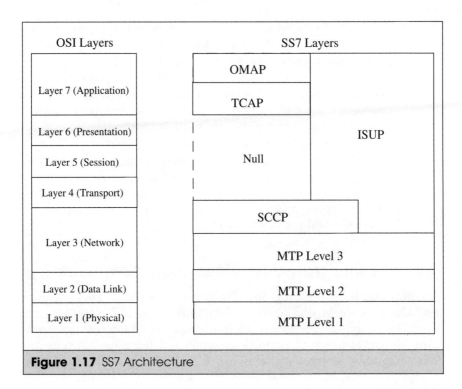

Figure 1.17 SS7 Architecture

setup, management, and clearing between telephone users. The SS7 network is an overlay network that provides user access to the telephone network. It supports a range of applications including the intelligent network, integrated services digital network, and the mobile cellular telephone network. Its architecture is organized into **parts,** each of which may be associated with functions of more than one OSI layer. Figure 1.17 shows how the SS7 layers map into the OSI reference model.

The functions performed in these parts are as follows:

- **Message Transfer Part** (MTP): This part has three levels and takes care of transferring messages, thereby fulfilling the role of layers 1 (physical) and 2 (data link) and part of layer 3 (network) of the OSI reference model.
- **Signaling Connection Control Part** (SCCP): This part provides the rest of the functions of the layer 3 of the OSI reference model. It also provides connectionless and connection-oriented services and address translation services. It uses the services of the MTP.
- **ISDN User Part** (ISUP): This part provides control for circuit-switched network services between exchanges. Sometimes it uses

the services of the SCCP; at other times it uses the services of the MTP directly thereby bypassing the SCCP.

- **Transaction Capabilities Application Part** (TCAP): This part maps into part of the application layer (layer 7) of the OSI reference model. It provides non-circuit related information transfer capabilities. It is especially used to query the necessary database for an 800/888/900 number translation in intelligent networks. The TCAP uses the services of the SCCP.

- **Operations, Maintenance and Administration Part** (OMAP): This part provides procedures required to monitor, coordinate, and control all the network resources needed to realize an SS7-based communication. It maps into a part of the application layer of the OSI reference model.

1.3 The Integrated Services Digital Network

A communication network provides services to users. These services include the transmission of voice, data, and video. The telephone network is a circuit-switched network that is optimized for voice transmission. A packet-switched network is optimized for data transmission. The **integrated services digital network** (ISDN) is a network that supports voice, data, and video services. It is expected to eliminate the need for separate networks for the different services and integrate them into one network. ISDN provides two types of services (or interfaces): the **basic rate interface** (BRI) and the **primary rate interface** (PRI).

BRI consists of two full-duplex 64-kbps bearer (B) channels and one full-duplex 16-kbps data (D) channel for a total of 144 kbps. (The D channel is also called the **delta channel**.) This service is sometimes known as the 2B+D service and is expected to meet the needs of most individual users and small businesses. PRI consists of 23 full-duplex 64-kbps B channels and one full-duplex 64-kbps D channel for a total of 1536 kbps. (In Europe, PRI consists of 30 64-kbps B channels and one 64-kbps D channel for a total of 1984 kbps.) PRI is also called the 23B+D service (or 30B+D service in Europe) and is designed for corporate use. In both BRI and PRI, the B channels can be used for voice or data, and the D channel can be used for signaling and for packet data transmission.

1.3.1 ISDN Reference Configuration

ISDN reference configuration is a conceptual configuration that helps us to identify the various possible physical user access arrangements to an ISDN [11]. There are two aspects of a reference configuration: **functional groups** and **reference points**. An ISDN functional group is a set of functions that may be needed in ISDN user access arrangements.

The functions may be performed in one or more pieces of equipment. An ISDN reference point is a conceptual interface between two functional groups. Sometimes a reference point may correspond to a physical interface between pieces of equipment; at other times there may not be any physical interface that corresponds to the reference point.

The ISDN reference configuration defines two broad classes of functional groups: **network termination** functional groups and **terminal equipment** functional groups. Terminal equipment devices are end-user devices, such as digital and analog telephones. Network termination devices provide a connection from a terminal equipment device to the ISDN. There are three types of terminal equipment functional groups and two types of network termination functional groups. These five types of functional groups are defined as follows:

- **Network termination 1** (NT1): This is a functional group that includes functions that are equivalent to layer 1 (physical layer) of the OSI reference model. NT1 allows entry to the public network. It represents the termination of the physical connection between the customer site and the local exchange and is responsible for such functions as layer 1 line performance monitoring, timing, and layer 1 multiplexing.
- **Network termination 2** (NT2): This is a functional group that provides local switching and multiplexing service. An NT2 device is an intelligent device that may include various levels of functionality up to layer 3 of the OSI reference model. Examples of NT2 devices include the PBX, multiplexer, host computers, and terminal controllers. NT2 devices are generally optional devices which may be used only in the basic rate interface environments.
- **Terminal equipment type 1** (TE1): This is a functional group that provides ISDN-specific functions. TE1 devices are ISDN-compatible terminals that utilize ISDN protocols and support ISDN services. They include videophones, ISDN telephones, and ISDN workstations.
- **Terminal equipment type 2** (TE2): This is a functional group that provides non-ISDN-specific functions. A TE2 device is a non-ISDN compatible device such as an analog telephone or a personal computer, and is connected to ISDN via a terminal adapter.
- **Terminal adapter** (TA): This is a functional group that enables non-ISDN equipment (TE2) to communicate with the network. A TA device provides any necessary protocol conversion to enable a TE2 device to be attached to an ISDN interface.

ISDN reference points define the communication protocols between different functional groups. There are four types of reference points:

- **Reference point R:** This is the interface between a non-ISDN terminal device (TE2) and a terminal adapter.
- **Reference point S:** This is the interface between an ISDN terminal device (TE1 or TA) and a network termination equipment (NT1 or NT2).
- **Reference point T:** This is the interface between customer site equipment (NT2) and a local loop termination (NT1). If NT2 is absent, the interface between the ISDN terminal device (TE1 or TA) is referred to as an **S/T reference point**. In this case NT1 and NT2 functions are merged in the same equipment.
- **Reference point U:** This is the interface between the local loop termination (NT1) and the local exchange. If the physical NT1 device is considered to be owned by the network service provider, reference point U does not exist. This is apparently the ITU-T view since it does not have any standard for the U reference point. However, in the United States, the reference point U is recognized as a valid reference point.

Figure 1.18 shows the reference configuration with the functional groups and reference points. Note that up to eight ISDN terminal devices (TE1 or TA) can be connected to the network termination equipment (NT2) via a passive bus (or S bus) in a basic rate interface system. For example, an ISDN telephone, an ISDN FAX machine, and an ISDN workstation may be attached to the same basic rate interface. Devices on the bus use an arbitration method called **TE arbitration** to listen to the bus and identify a message requesting a service each device can provide. When a device identifies a message requesting a service it can provide, it connects to a B channel.

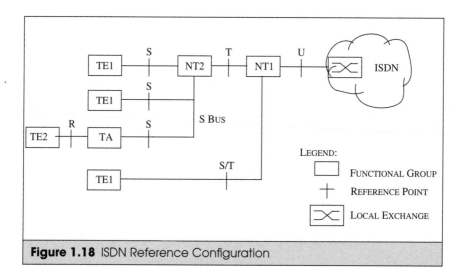

Figure 1.18 ISDN Reference Configuration

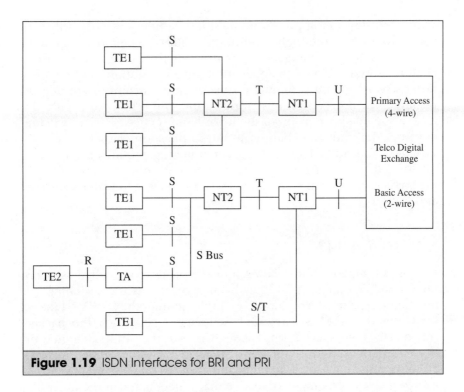

Figure 1.19 ISDN Interfaces for BRI and PRI

Figure 1.19 shows how the ISDN reference configuration is realized for both the basic rate interface (BRI) and the primary rate interface (PRI). BRI access terminates at the Telco central office as a 2-wire line while PRI access terminates as a 4-wire line.

1.4 Broadband ISDN

While BRI and PRI bit rates can support a wide range of services, there are emerging services that require higher bit rates than BRI and PRI provide. These services include multimedia communication, high-definition television, high resolution image communication (such as medical images), video retrieval, and video conferencing. The need to support these services, which are often referred to as **broadband services,** has led to a new ISDN service called the **broadband ISDN** (B-ISDN) which is expected to support up to 622 Mbps. The BRI and PRI services defined in the previous section are now called the **narrowband ISDN** (N-ISDN).

The high bit rate requirement of the B-ISDN demands a mode of information transfer that is different from the traditional circuit mode and packet mode. In circuit-switched digital networks, bandwidth consists of fixed-size channels (or slots). When an application needs more bandwidth than that provided by one slot, more slots are allocated to it.

With a few slots per application, the slot scheduling can be easily managed. However, at the high bandwidths required by the broadband services, the slot scheduling becomes difficult to manage. Also, since a channel is dedicated to an application for the duration of the application's session, circuit switching results in an inefficient use of network resources for non-continuous bit rate applications that are expected to form a sizeable proportion of the broadband services. Packet switching does not dedicate any channel to any application; rather, it provides variable bandwidth. However, packet switching requires a lot of software-based processing to do error checking and flow control. This introduces extra delay that makes it unsuitable for delay-sensitive applications.

1.5 Why ATM?

Because of the above limitations, a new transfer mode called **asynchronous transfer mode** (ATM) has been accepted as the switching and information transmission mode for implementing the B-ISDN. Like the packet mode, ATM is a packet-based scheme in which the packets, called **cells,** have a fixed size. Through statistical multiplexing, network resources are used more efficiently than in a circuit-switched network. However, unlike packet switching, and as in circuit switching, ATM provides a guaranteed quality of service that is negotiated at the beginning of a session. It reserves network resources (but does not dedicate them to any session) to meet the negotiated quality of service.

The goal of this book is to provide a basic understanding of ATM networks and the services that are expected to be provided over an ATM network.

1.6 ATM Applications

Both the telephone companies (Telcos) and the business community have invested very heavily in both physical networking infrastructures and applications that run on these networks. Thus, it is not possible, at least in the short run, to scrap the current networking technologies in favor of any new technology such as the ATM network. This means that the ATM network, which the Telcos originally intended to be used as a public carrier network for providing broadband services, will serve mainly as a backbone network for connecting the legacy networks in the short run. This observation is borne out by the activities of the ATM Forum, especially in the specification of such services as ATM LAN emulation and multiprotocol over ATM (MPOA). These services are described in later chapters.

As stated earlier, the Telcos originally intended that the ATM network be used to provide broadband services over the public carrier network. However, with the formation of the ATM Forum, the ATM market has ceased to be a single market. Instead, it has evolved into three separate markets, each with different requirements and characteristics. These markets are:

- ATM LAN
- ATM Backbone (or ATM WAN)
- ATM Central Office (CO)

One of the characteristics of these three markets is the type of ATM switches found in them. An ATM LAN switch has a capacity of up to 2.5 gigabits per second (Gbps) and can be used as a stand-alone switch. It is used to interconnect legacy LANs, hubs, and ATM-capable workstations. Typically, an ATM LAN switch has a low port density. ATM LAN switches are the key to bringing ATM to the desktop. An ATM LAN switch is sometimes referred to as a **workgroup ATM switch**.

An ATM WAN is a backbone enterprise network that interconnects the corporate ATM LANs. An ATM WAN switch has a capacity that ranges from 2.5 Gbps to 10 Gbps, and has moderate to high port density.

A public carrier network supports a large number of user connections and a variety of services including frame relay and circuit emulation service. It is also capable of connecting a large number of private enterprise networks. Consequently, an ATM CO switch has a capacity of more than 10 Gbps with very high port density. Figure 1.20 shows the relationships of the different ATM switches.

1.7 ATM Standardization

The ITU-T Study Group 13 (formerly the CCITT Study Group XVIII) began developing standards for broadband ISDN in 1985. The original goal was to develop a high-capacity wide area network technology for the introduction of broadband services at rates of 150 Mbps and higher. However, since then, the data communications industry has helped to broaden the areas of application of ATM, as discussed in the previous section.

Several organizations have contributed to the standardization of ATM. Foremost among these organizations are the ITU-T, ANSI, ETSI, and the ATM Forum.

The **International Telecommunications Union** (ITU) is a United Nations agency that deals with telecommunications regulation, standardization, coordination, and development. One of its subunits (or sectors, as they are known) is the ITU Telecommunication Standardization Sector (or ITU-T, which was formerly called the CCITT). The function of the ITU-T is to facilitate the development of global standards for telecommunications. It carries out this function through study groups,

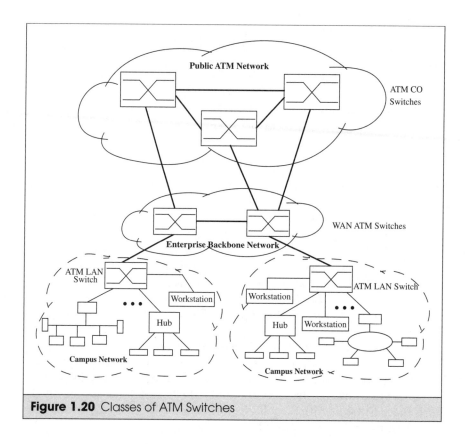

Figure 1.20 Classes of ATM Switches

which in turn are made up of working parties. Study Group 13 is responsible for B-ISDN and has issued several ATM-related documents called recommendations. (There are two other sectors of the ITU: the ITU Radiocummunication Sector, and the ITU Telecommunication Development Sector.)

The **American National Standards Institute** (ANSI) is responsible for defining US standards for the information processing industry. It is a non-profit, non-governmental organization that is supported by trade organizations, professional societies such as the Institute of Electrical and Electronics Engineers (IEEE), and corporations. It works through many committees that are actually responsible for developing standards. The committee T1 is responsible for producing U.S. national telecommunications standards. ANSI is the U.S. member of the International Standards Organization, which develops standards for communication between cooperating data processing systems, and the U.S. representative to the International Electrotechnical Commission, which promotes safety, compatibility, interchangeability, and acceptability of international electrical products. Most of the ANSI standards are proposed to the ITU-T for consideration as ITU-T recommendations.

The **European Telecommunication Standards Institute** (ETSI) is an independent organization that was established in 1988 to set telecommunication standards for the European Union. Its approved specifications are called European Telecommunication Standards that may be used as a technical basis for regulation within the European Union. Most of ETSI specifications are proposed to the ITU-T for consideration as ITU-T recommendations.

The **ATM Forum** (ATMF) is an international organization formed in 1991 with the objective of accelerating the use of ATM products and services through interoperability specifications. It consists of over 700 member companies. It has a technical committee that works with other standards bodies, such as the ITU-T and ANSI, to select standards, resolve differences among standards, and recommend new standards when existing ones are absent or inappropriate [12].

1.8 Summary

This chapter presented an overview of the development of telecommunications. This chapter also introduced you to telecommunications and data communication network architectures. It included an overview of the ISDN and discussed the rationale for and applications of ATM. The following chapters will discuss the different aspects of the ATM network and services.

CHAPTER 2

ATM Basics

2.1 Introduction

Chapter 1 described ATM as a connection-oriented, high-speed switching and multiplexing scheme for B-ISDN. One of the advantages of ATM is that it is a standards-based technology, and this makes interoperability of ATM equipment possible. Another advantage of the technology is its ability to handle all traffic types in a homogeneous manner. The same method is used to handle voice, video, multimedia, and LAN traffic. To support this multi-service environment, ATM attempts to resolve most of the requirements that are specific to any given traffic type at the edges of the ATM network.

This implies that ATM enjoys the strengths of both time-division multiplexing (TDM) and statistical multiplexing while avoiding their weaknesses. As in TDM, ATM offers guaranteed service with resources allocated to meet the desired quality of service. Similarly, as in statistical multiplexing, ATM uses network resources efficiently. However, unlike TDM, it does not dedicate bandwidth to any application, and unlike statistical multiplexing, which is not appropriate for real-time applications, ATM can handle both real-time and non-real-time applications.

This chapter will examine the B-ISDN architecture, which is key to understanding the rest of the discussion on ATM.

2.2 B-ISDN Architecture

The B-ISDN is logically organized in a layered architecture called the **B-ISDN protocol reference model** (PRM), which in turn is organized into three planes:

1. The **user plane** deals with the transfer of user information, including mechanisms for flow control and error recovery.
2. The **control plane** is responsible for call and connection control functions, particularly the signaling function that enables the setup, supervision, and release of a call or connection.
3. The **management plane** is responsible for network supervision.

The protocol reference model is usually represented as a three-dimensional diagram to reflect these three planes, as shown in Figure 2.1.

The user plane and the control plane consist of three layers: the ATM adaptation layer, the ATM layer, and the physical layer. The ATM adaptation layer (AAL) is the highest of these three layers and the physical layer is the lowest lower. The two planes have the same ATM and physical layers but different ATM adaptation layers.

- The **ATM adaptation layer** ensures appropriate service characteristics and divides all data types into 48-octet units (called **payloads**) that are passed on to the ATM layer. The AAL for the control plane is called the **signaling AAL** (SAAL). The ATM adaptation layer is covered in greater detail in Chapter 4.
- The **ATM layer** takes the payload sent by the adaptation layer and adds five octets of header information to form a **cell**. The header information ensures that the cell is sent on the right connection.

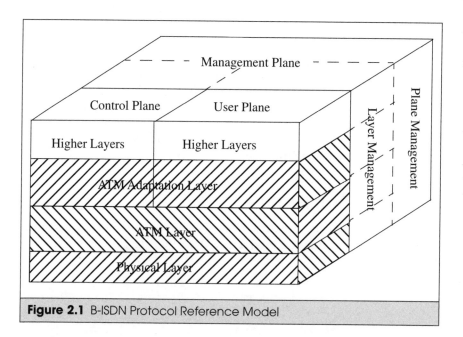

Figure 2.1 B-ISDN Protocol Reference Model

- The **physical layer** defines the electrical and/or optical characteristics and network interfaces and puts the bits on the wire. The physical layer is subdivided into two sublayers:

  1. The **transmission convergence** (TC) sublayer, which performs functions that are independent of the physical medium including transmission frame generation and recovery, placing cells into and extracting cells from SONET frames, identifying and recovering cell boundaries, cell header error processing, and inserting and extracting empty cells.

  2. The **physical medium dependent** (PMD) sublayer, which performs functions that are dependent on the medium such as bit timing and line coding. It is the lower of the two sublayers.

The management plane includes two types of functions: layer management and plane management. **Layer management** has a layered structure and each of its layers handles the specific operations and maintenance (OAM) information flows for the corresponding layers. (OAM flows are discussed in Chapter 6.) Plane management is not layered and its task is to provide coordination among all the planes.

In terms of packet and cell flows in the network, Figure 2.2 shows how the interfaces are defined.

2.3 ATM Cell Header

As stated earlier, an ATM cell has a 48-octet information field (or payload) and a 5-octet header, as shown in Figure 2.3.

The header appended by the ATM layer is made up of several fields as shown in Figure 2.4. These fields are the generic flow control, virtual

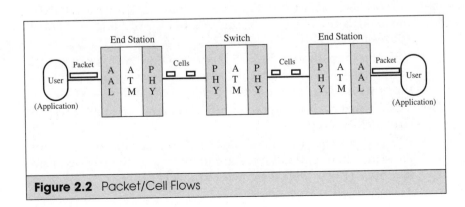

Figure 2.2 Packet/Cell Flows

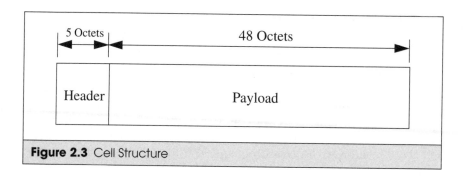

Figure 2.3 Cell Structure

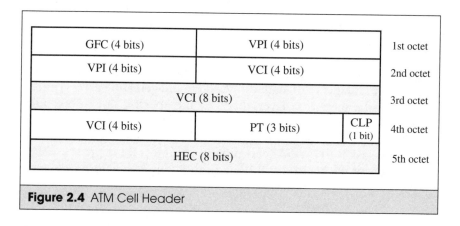

Figure 2.4 ATM Cell Header

path identifier, virtual channel identifier, payload type, and cell loss priority.

The specific functions of the fields are as follows:

- **GFC:** Generic flow control (4 bits) is not defined yet for a user-network interface (UNI). For a network-network interface (NNI), this field is used as part of the VPI field, providing additional addressing capacity.
- **VPI:** Virtual path identifier (8 bits) allows up to $2^8 = 256$ virtual paths. Each VP contains virtual channels, a virtual path is a bundle of virtual channels with the same VPI but different VCIs.
- **VCI:** Virtual channel identifier (16 bits) allows up to $2^{16} = 65,536$ virtual channels in one VP.
- **PT:** Payload type (3 bits) allows ATM to carry up to 8 types of payload. These payload types are identified by the **payload type identifier** (PTI). Table 2.1 contains the PTI coding.

Table 2.1 PTI Coding

PTI Coding (MSB first)	Interpretation
000	User data cell, congestion not experienced, SDU-type = 0 (i.e., beginning or continuation of SAR-SDU in AAL type 5)
001	User data cell, congestion not experienced, SDU-type = 1 (i.e., end of SAR-SDU in AAL type 5)
010	User data cell, congestion experienced, SDU-type = 0
011	User data cell, congestion experienced, SDU-type = 1
100	OAM F5 segment associated cell
101	OAM F5 end-to-end associated cell
110	Resource management (RM) cell (used in traffic management)
111	Reserved for future functions

Essentially, the most significant bit (bit 3) is used to distinguish data cells from OAM cells; it is 0 for data cells and 1 for OAM cells. For data cells, bit 2 is used to indicate congestion; it is 0 if no congestion is experienced and 1 otherwise. Finally, for data cells, bit 1 is 0 for service data unit (SDU) type 0 cells and 1 for SDU type 1 cells.

- **CLP:** Cell loss priority (1 bit) is used to determine the eligibility of a cell for discard when the network is congested. If CLP = 1, the cell may be discarded; otherwise, it may not be discarded.
- **HEC:** Header error control (8 bits) is used for error correction on the other bits in the header. The HEC enables an ATM switch to detect multiple errors and correct single errors.

A user-network interface (UNI) cell is structured as shown in Figure 2.5.

Since ATM is a connection-oriented technology, a unidirectional communication capability used for the transport of ATM cells is called a **virtual channel**. The combination of the VPI and VCI is a label used to identify the virtual channel to which a cell belongs. As a result, cells belonging to the same virtual channel have the same VPI and VCI. This means that from a networking point of view, the ATM layer can then be

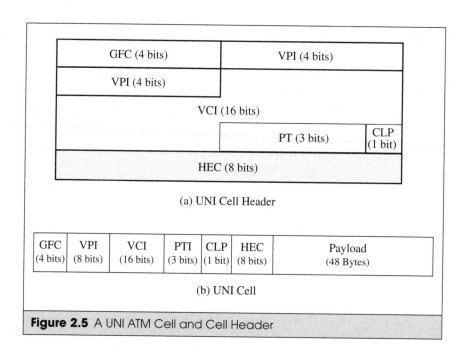

(a) UNI Cell Header

(b) UNI Cell

Figure 2.5 A UNI ATM Cell and Cell Header

perceived as being divided into two hierarchical levels: a virtual channel level (the higher level) and a virtual path level (the lower layer). Figure 2.6 illustrates the ATM layer.

The GFC field is not used in UNI cells. However, it is used as part of the VPI field for NNI cells, giving a total of 12 bits for the VPI field (or $2^{12} = 4096$ VPIs). The NNI cell is structured as shown in Figure 2.7. One advantage of this is that the number of virtual paths that can be defined at the NNI level increases from 256 (when only 8 bits are used: $2^8 = 256$) to 4096. This provides a 15-fold increase in the number of

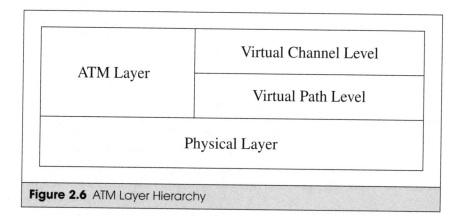

Figure 2.6 ATM Layer Hierarchy

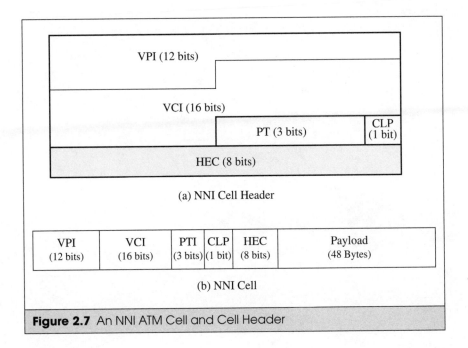

Figure 2.7 An NNI ATM Cell and Cell Header

virtual paths that an interexchange service provider can specify at each ATM switch.

2.4 Summary

This chapter presented an overview of the B-ISDN architecture, including the cell header formats. The header for the user-network interface frames is slightly different from that for the network-network interface. The former has an unused GFC field while the latter incorporates the GFC into its VPI field, thereby permitting more virtual paths to be defined between two networks.

ATM Networking

3.1 Introduction

An ATM network consists of a set of ATM switches interconnected by point-to-point ATM links. The switches support two kinds of interfaces: user-network interface (UNI) and network-network interface (NNI). UNI connects an ATM end system to the switch and NNI connects two ATM switches belonging to different network systems.

Since ATM networks are connection-oriented, a virtual circuit must be established before data can be routed from source to destination. As discussed in Chapter 2, ATM uses the concepts of **virtual channels** (VCs) and **virtual paths** (VPs) to accomplish routing in the network. A VC, identified by a **virtual channel identifier** (VCI), is a connection between two communicating ATM entities. It consists of a concatenation of one or more ATM links. A VC provides a certain quality of service. A VP, identified by a **virtual path identifier** (VPI), is a group of VCs between two endpoints. VPI and VCI have only local significance and are usually remapped at each switch. Figure 3.1 shows the relationship between a physical link, VPs, and VCs.

Virtual channels can be established in two ways:

- **Permanent virtual channel** (PVC): This is a connection established by a network operator in which appropriate VPI/VCI values are programmed for a given source and a given destination. Thus, PVCs are established by provisioning and usually last a long time (months, years).
- **Switched virtual channel** (SVC): An SVC is established automatically through a signaling protocol and lasts for only a short time (minutes, hours).

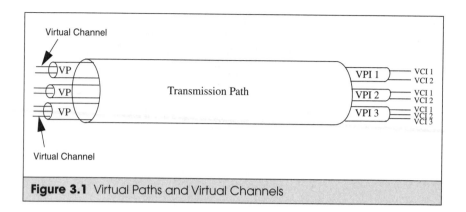

Figure 3.1 Virtual Paths and Virtual Channels

Several VPI/VCI pairs have been reserved for special functions. These are [13]:

- (VPI, VCI) = (0, 5): for signaling
- (VPI, VCI) = (0, 16): for integrated local management interface (ILMI) (see Chapter 6)
- (VPI, VCI) = (0, 17): for the LAN emulation configuration server (LECS) (see Chapter 9)
- (VPI, VCI) = (0, 18): for private network-network interface (PNNI) Hello protocol (see Chapter 8)
- (VPI, VCI) = (0, 19) and (0, 20): reserved, but not yet used

3.2 VP and VC Switching

An ATM network can provide either a virtual path level service or a virtual channel level service, or both. In a network that provides a virtual path level service, when a switch receives a cell with given virtual path identifier and virtual channel identifier, it does a table lookup to determine how the virtual path identifier value is to be remapped for forwarding to the next switch or end system. The virtual channel identifier value is not remapped. This type of switching is called **virtual path switching** (VP switching).

Similarly, in a network that provides a virtual channel level service, when a switch receives a cell with a given virtual path identifier and a virtual channel identifier, it assigns new virtual path identifier and virtual channel identifier values to the cell before forwarding it to the next switch or end system. This type of switching is called **virtual channel switching** (VC switching). Figure 3.2 illustrates the concepts of VP switching and VC switching. In Figure 3.2a, the virtual channels retain their virtual channel identifiers after a virtual path's virtual path identi-

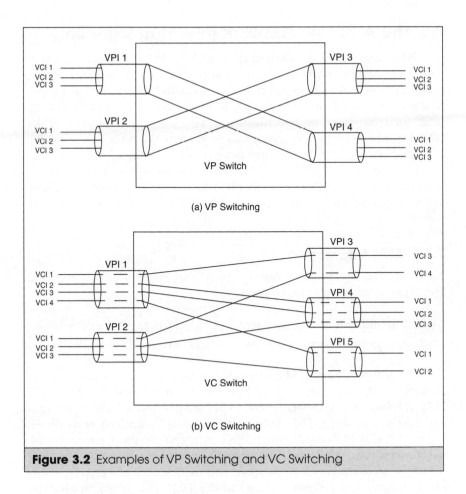

Figure 3.2 Examples of VP Switching and VC Switching

fier has been remapped to a new value. On the other hand, in Figure 3.2b there is both a virtual path identifier and virtual channel identifier remapping for each virtual channel.

A virtual channel essentially identifies a unidirectional facility for transporting ATM cells. A **virtual channel link** (VC link) is a unidirectional facility for transporting ATM cells between two consecutive ATM entities where a VCI value is assigned and remapped or removed. This implies that a VC link is defined between two consecutive VC switches and between an ATM end system and a VC switch. A concatenation of VC links is called a **virtual channel connection** (VCC). Similarly, a VP link is a unidirectional facility for transporting ATM cells between two consecutive ATM entities where the VPI values are assigned and remapped or removed. Thus, a VP link is defined between an ATM end system and a VC switch, between a VC switch and a VP switch, and between two consecutive VP switches. A concatenation of VP links is called a **virtual path connection** (VPC).

3.3 The ATM User-Network Interface Signaling

The ATM network is a switched network and therefore operates in a connection-oriented manner. It must allow the user (or end system) to establish **switched-on-demand** connections. This is the role of **signaling**. At the user-network interface (UNI) level, the ATM Forum has issued a series of UNI signaling specifications. The latest specification is the UNI 4.0. This section will review this version of the ATM UNI; Section 3.3.3 discusses how it differs from two previous versions.

In order to establish a connection between two end systems, the two end systems must be uniquely identifiable by the network. **Addressing** is a mechanism by which end systems can be identified in a unique manner.

3.3.1 ATM Addressing

An ATM address identifies one or more end systems in the network. Two types of addresses can be used:

1. The **individual address** identifies only a single ATM end system.
2. The **group address** identifies one or more ATM end systems.

The format of an ATM address for endsystems in private networks is modeled after that of the OSI Network Service Access Point (NSAP) [14]. It is hierarchically structured to permit distributed administration and efficient routing. The abstract structure of an address is shown in Figure 3.3. It is a 20-octet format that consists of two main parts: the **initial domain part** (IDP) and the **domain specific part** (DSP). The IDP uniquely specifies an administrative authority which has responsibility for allocating and assigning values to the DSP. The DSP contains the address determined by the network authority. Each of the two parts has different components.

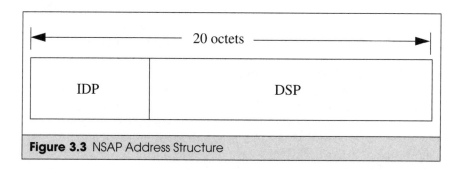

Figure 3.3 NSAP Address Structure

3.3.1.1 IDP Components

The IDP has two components: the **authority format identifier** (AFI) and the **initial domain identifier** (IDI). The AFI is a 1-octet field that identifies the network addressing authority responsible for allocating values to the IDI. The following codes are specified:

39 = Data Country Code (DCC) ATM format

47 = International Code Designator (ICD) ATM format

45 = E.164 ATM format

All other code values are reserved.

The IDI is a 2-octet field that specifies the addressing domain and network addressing authority that is responsible for allocating the values of the DSP. It is interpreted according to the values of the AFI and identifies the following formats:

- **ICD:** A 2-octet field which specifies an international organization. Codes are allocated by the British Standards Institute, which is the registration authority for the ISO 6523 [15].
- **DCC:** A two-octet field that specifies the country in which the address is registered. The codes are given in ISO 3166 [16].
- **E.164** [17]: An 8-octet field which specifies ISDN numbers that include telephone numbers.

The IDC and DCC formats are useful for organizations that wish to maintain a private numbering plan that is organizationally based. The E.164 format is useful for organizations that wish to use the existing largely geographically based public ISDN/telephony numbering format. Figure 3.4 shows the IDP structure.

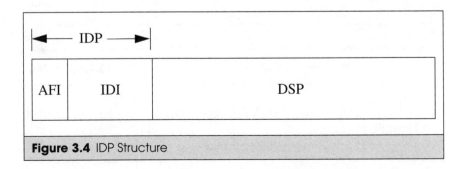

Figure 3.4 IDP Structure

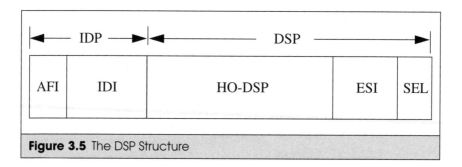

Figure 3.5 The DSP Structure

3.3.1.2 DSP Components

The DSP is divided into two parts: the high-order DSP (HO-DSP) and the low-order DSP that consists of the end system identifier (ESI) and the selector (SEL). Figure 3.5 illustrates the structure of the DSP.

HO-DSP contains subfields that describe a hierarchical addressing that facilitates hierarchical routing through interconnected ATM networks. One example of the use of the HO-DSP is the US GOSIP format [18]. This falls within the ICD format with IDI = 0005. The HO-DSP subfields for this format are shown in Figure 3.6, and the components are as follows:

- **DFI** (Domain Format Identifier, 1 octet): Specifies the structure, semantics, and administrative requirements for the remainder of the address.
- **AA** (Administrative Authority, 3 octets): Specifies the organization that the National Institute of Standards and Technology (NIST) has delegated the authority to suballocate addresses in the remainder of the DSP.
- **RSVD** (Reserved, 2 octets): Not currently used.
- **RD** (Routing Domain, 2 octets): Specifies a unique domain within the prefix ICD+DFI+AA.

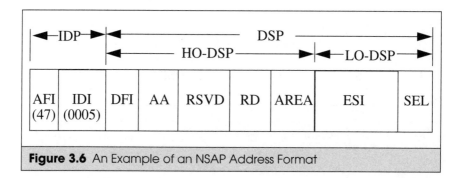

Figure 3.6 An Example of an NSAP Address Format

- **AREA** (Area, 2 octets): Identifies a unique area within an RD.
- **ESI** (End System Identifier, 6 octets): Identifies a unique end system within an area; it is usually the IEEE 802 MAC address.
- **SEL** (Selector, 1 octet): Not used for ATM routing but can be used by end systems to specify the protocol entities in the upper layers of the end system that have to receive the traffic.

There is no consensus on which addressing scheme is the best scheme. However, a majority of the vendors use either the ICD or the DCC format. The problem with using the E.164 format (in the U.S. in particular) is that when the area code changes, as they have been lately, all the switches with the E.164 AFI format need to be reprogrammed with the new area code. This may be the reason why the other two schemes are used by most vendors.

3.3.2 UNI Signaling 4.0

UNI signaling 4.0 (or UNI 4.0) [13] is based on the ITU-T Q.2931 [19] and Q.2110 [20] recommendations. It is an extension of UNI 3.1 [21] and is backward-compatible with UNI 3.1. The basic functions provided by UNI 4.0 include the following:

- Point-to-point call support
- Point-to-multipoint call support
- Switched virtual path service
- Leaf-initiated join capability, whereby a leaf may join a point-to-multipoint connection with or without intervention from the root of the connection.
- ATM Anycast capability, the ability to allow an application to request a point-to-point connection to an end system that is part of an ATM group. (UNI 3.1 and ITU-T Q.2931 support point-to-point connections that indicate a single end system.)
- Group addressing, a capability to identify one or more ATM end systems with one address.
- Proxy signaling, a feature that allows a user, called the **proxy signaling agent,** to perform signaling for one or more users that do not support signaling. It can be used to allow a high-end ATM equipment to support multiple physical interfaces that share the same ATM address.
- Multiple signaling channels, a capability that supports multiple users on a single UNI which requires support for multiple ILMI channels (one for each signaling channel). This effectively creates "virtual UNIs," many of which can exist on a single UNI or port.

- Frame discard support
- ABR signaling for point-to-point calls
- Traffic parameter negotiation
- Signaling of individual QoS parameters
- Supplementary services including direct dialing in (DDI), calling line identification presentation (CLIP), calling line identification restriction (CLIR), connected line identification presentation, connected line identification restriction, subaddressing, and user-to-user signaling.

The process of sending information from a source to a destination involves three phases:

- Call/connection setup phase
- Data transfer phase
- Call/connection release phase

3.3.2.1 Call/Connection Setup

The following are the steps involved in the call/connection setup phase:

1. The calling party (i.e., the source end system) initiates a call/connection setup by sending a SETUP message to the source switch. Each SETUP message contains the source and destination addresses as well as a set of **information elements** (IEs), which are parameters that quantitatively describe aspects of the service that the user is requesting from the network.

2. When the source switch receives the message, it analyzes the message to determine if it can service the call based on the declared QoS. If it can, the switch sends the SETUP message to the succeeding switch on the path to the destination. It then returns a CALL PROCEEDING message to the calling party to acknowledge the SETUP message. If the switch cannot service the call, it enters the call release phase.

3. Any transit switch that receives the SETUP message and can service the call will send the message to the succeeding switch and return a CALL PROCEEDING message to the preceding switch. Otherwise, it enters the call release phase.

4. When the destination switch receives the SETUP message and determines that it can service the call, it sends the message to the destination and returns the CALL PROCEEDING message to the preceding switch.

5. When the destination end system receives the message, it returns the CALL PROCEEDING message to the destination switch and processes the connection request. If it accepts the message, it

sends a CONNECT message to the source end system via the destination switch. The latter sends the message to the preceding switch and returns a CONNECT ACK message to the destination end system.

6. Any switch that receives the CONNECT message will forward it to the preceding switch and return a CONNECT ACK message to the succeeding switch.

7. When the source end system receives the CONNECT message, it returns a CONNECT ACK message to the source switch, and this completes the call/connection setup phase.

Figure 3.7 shows an example of the above information flow where there is only one transit switch.

As stated above, the SETUP message contains a set of IEs that are used to determine how the call/connection will be handled. Some of these IEs are mandatory and others are optional. The mandatory IEs include the ATM traffic descriptor IE, the broadband bearer capability IE, and the QoS parameter IE. Other IEs include the minimum acceptable rate IE, the AAL parameter IE (that specifies the AAL type), and the end-to-end transit delay IE.

3.3.2.2 Data Transfer

After the call/connection setup phase has been completed, the source and destination can exchange information over the established VCC.

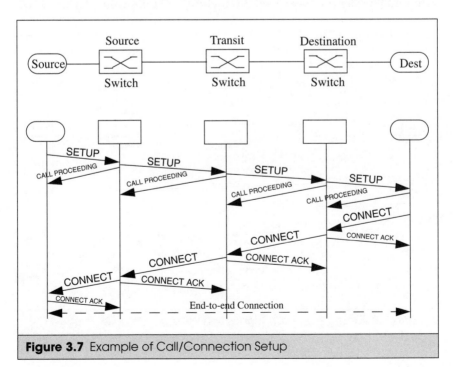

Figure 3.7 Example of Call/Connection Setup

3.3.2.3 Call/Connection Release

This phase is initiated when either party sends a RELEASE message to the network. Assume that the source initiates the call/connection release. The sequence of information flow is as follows:

1. The source end system sends a RELEASE message to the source switch.
2. The source switch sends the message to the transit switch and returns a RELEASE ACK message to the source end system.
3. When the transit switch receives the RELEASE message, it forwards it to the destination switch and returns a RELEASE COMPLETE message to the source switch.
4. When the destination switch receives the RELEASE message, it sends it to the destination end system and returns the RELEASE COMPLETE message to the destination switch.
5. The destination end system returns a RELEASE ACK to the destination switch, and this completes the release phase.

Figure 3.8 illustrates the above process.

3.3.3 UNI Signaling 3.0 and UNI Signaling 3.1

UNI signaling version 3.0 [22] was ratified in 1993 and is based on the ITU-T Q.93B recommendations [23] for its support of switched virtual circuits. The highlights of UNI 3.0 include the following:

- It supports the E.164 address format as well as private network address format based on the OSI layer 3 NSAP. The ATM switch

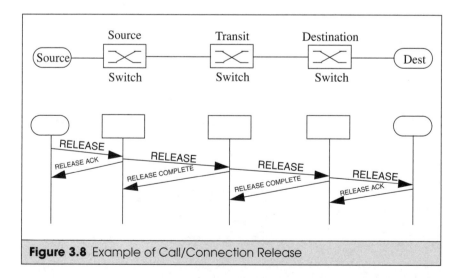

Figure 3.8 Example of Call/Connection Release

supplies the high-order portion of the address while the end system fills the 6-byte station ID, usually an 802-style MAC address. This provides hierarchy and unique automatic address assignment.

- It permits quality of service (QoS) parameters to be passed in the connection setup message for each virtual circuit. QoS parameters include peak cell rate, peak burst length, and sustainable cell rate.
- It does not permit negotiation of QoS parameters; it is essentially an all-or-nothing issue in which the ATM network either accepts all the parameters or rejects all of them if it cannot meet any QoS requirement.

UNI 3.1 is a modification of the UNI 3.0 and is based on the ITU-T Q.2931 and Q.2110 recommendations rather than Q.93B. Q.2110 defines the Service-Specific Connection-Oriented Protocol (SSCOP) which provides for reliable transfer of signaling data. Because UNI 3.0 and UNI 3.1 use incompatible SSCOPs, the two are not compatible. UNI 3.1 supports point-to-multipoint connection setup. It allows root-initiated joins whereby a root node can set up a point-to-multipoint connection and later add leaf nodes to the connection.

3.4 Summary

This chapter described the two levels of multiplexing hierarchy defined for the ATM network: the virtual path (VP) and the virtual channel (VC). A physical link may support several VPs, and each VP has a virtual path identifier (VPI). Similarly, a VP is essentially a bundle of VCs, and each VC has a virtual channel identifier (VCI). At each switch, the VPI is translated (or remapped) into a new VPI. In some switches the VCIs in each VP remain intact during the process of VPI translation. Such switches that translate only VPIs are called VP switches. Similarly, in some switches the VCIs are translated along with the VPIs; such switches are called VC switches. There are hybrid switches that have the ability to translate some VCIs while leaving others intact.

Each end system that communicates over an ATM network is identified by a unique ATM address that is modeled after the OSI NSAP address format in private ATM networks. The address is hierarchically structured to permit efficient routing and distributed administration. Before one end system (the source) can communicate with another end system (the destination), the source must "talk" to the network. The network either has the end-to-end connection provisioned or has to establish one on demand. Provisioned connections are called permanent virtual channels (PVCs), and those established on demand are called switched virtual channels (SVCs). SVCs are established via signaling protocols. The ATM Forum has developed the UNI signaling protocols and the earliest is the UNI 3.0. This was based on the ITU-T Q.93B recommendations. A later version is the UNI 3.1 that is based on the ITU-T Q.2931 recommendations. However, it is not compatible with UNI 3.0. The latest version is the UNI 4.0 that provides more functionality than the UNI 3.1 and is backward compatible with UNI 3.1.

In public ATM networks, end systems are identified by means of E.164 numbers, as in the narrowband ISDN and current telephone systems.

ATM Traffic Classification

4.1 Introduction

There are several ways user traffic can be classified. Both the ITU-T and the ATM Forum have classified user traffic using different criteria. The different classification schemes are discussed in this chapter. This chapter will also discuss how the different classification schemes are interrelated.

4.2 User Service Classes

At the highest layer of the user plane, the ITU-T committee has identified three parameters for defining service classification. These are:

- Timing relation between source and destination (required or not required)
- Bit rate (constant or variable)
- Connection mode (connection-oriented or connectionless)

Based on these parameters, four feasible classes of user traffic can be distinguished:

- **Class A:** Connection-oriented constant bit rate (CBR) service, such as circuit emulation and CBR video
- **Class B:** Connection-oriented variable bit rate (VBR) service with a timing relation between the source and the destination, such as VBR video and audio

	Class A	Class B	Class C	Class D
Timing relation between source and destination	Required		Not required	
Bit rate	Constant	Variable		
Connection mode	Connection-oriented			Connectionless

Figure 4.1 Service Classification

- **Class C:** Connection-oriented VBR service without a timing relation between the source and the destination, such as connection-oriented file (i.e., data) transfer
- **Class D:** Connectionless VBR service, such as LAN data

These service classes are summarized in Figure 4.1.

4.3 ATM Adaptation Layer Traffic Types

The AAL supports all the four classes of service defined by the ITU-T. However, AAL functions are service-specific and were originally designated as AAL types 1 to 4 to correspond to the four service classes. Later on, AAL3 and AAL4 were merged into AAL3/4 and AAL5 was defined as a simpler and more efficient version of AAL3/4. These four types of AALs are defined as follows:

- **ATM Adaptation Layer Type 1:** CBR service, which allows ATM to emulate voice or DSn (n = 0, 1, or 3) traffic.
- **ATM Adaptation Layer Type 2:** VBR service with timing relation between the source and destination—presently no standards have been defined for the service.
- **ATM Adaptation Layer Type 3/4:** VBR service without timing relation between source and destination.
- **ATM Adaptation Layer Type 5:** Connectionless traffic.

The user plane protocol reference model is shown in Figure 4.2.

4.4 QoS Classes

Quality of service (QoS) refers to a set of user-perceivable ATM performance parameters that characterize the traffic over a given virtual connection. QoS parameters include the following:

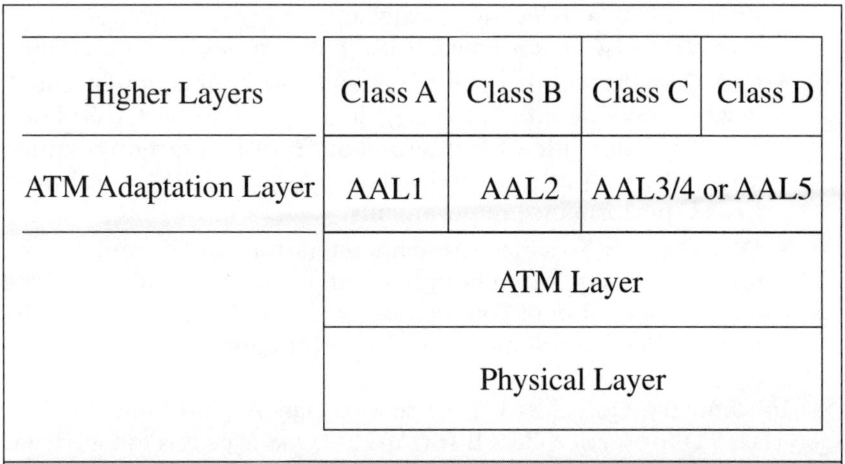

Higher Layers	Class A	Class B	Class C	Class D
ATM Adaptation Layer	AAL1	AAL2	AAL3/4 or AAL5	
	ATM Layer			
	Physical Layer			

Figure 4.2 User Plane Protocol Reference Model

- **Cell loss ratio** (CLR): The ratio of lost cells to the total number of transmitted cells.
- **Cell error ratio** (CER): The ratio of errored cells to the total cells transmitted.
- **Cell transfer delay** (CTD): The average time for a cell to be transferred from its source to its destination over a virtual connection.
- **Cell delay variation** (CDV): The difference between the actual transfer delay of an arbitrary cell and the expected transfer delay of that cell. The CDV is induced by buffering and cell scheduling at the different switches.
- **Cell misinsertion rate** (CMR): The ratio of the misinserted cells (i.e., those that arrive from the wrong source) to the total number of properly received cells per virtual connection.

ATM traffic can be classified into five QoS classes [24]:

- **QoS Class 0:** Refers to the best-effort service; no objective is specified for the performance parameters.
- **QoS Class 1:** Specifies the parameters for circuit emulation and CBR. It is a connection-oriented class that is supported by AAL1 and should yield performance comparable to that of current digital private line. It supports a QoS that will meet Class A performance requirements.
- **QoS Class 2:** Specifies parameters for VBR video and audio. It is also a connection-oriented, delay-dependent class that is supported by AAL2. It is intended for interoperation of packetized

video and audio teleconferencing and multimedia applications. It supports a QoS that will meet Class B performance requirements.

- **QoS Class 3:** Specifies the parameters for connection-oriented, delay-independent data transfer. It is supported by AAL3/4 and AAL5. It is intended for interoperation of connection-oriented protocols, such as frame relay. It supports a QoS that will meet Class C performance requirements.

- **QoS Class 4:** Specifies the parameters for connectionless data transfer. It is supported by either AAL3/4 or AAL5. It is intended for interoperation of connectionless protocols, such as IP. It supports a QoS that will meet Class D performance requirements.

In summary, QoS class 1 is for service class A (and hence AAL1), QoS class 2 is for service class B (or AAL2), QoS class 3 is for service C (which may be AAL3/4 of AAL5), and QoS class 4 is for service class 4 (which may also be AAL3/4 or AAL5).

4.5 ATM Service Categories

ATM networks are expected to support several traffic types. As described in the previous section, these traffic types come from applications that have been labelled Class A, ..., Class D. At the AAL they are labelled AAL types 1, 3/4, and 5. The ATM Forum Traffic Management sub-working group has developed a more comprehensive service architecture that introduces the possibility for the user to select specific combinations of traffic and performance parameters. The rationale for this architecture is the following: While the choice of an appropriate AAL permits most of the requirements specific to an application to be resolved at the edge of the network, the ATM layer behavior should not rely on either the AAL protocols or the higher layer protocols that are application specific [25].

The service categories accommodate the fact that ATM handles a heterogeneous traffic mix. Thus, the goal is to ensure that network resources are allocated in a fair way for each traffic component. An ATM service category represents a class of ATM connections that have homogeneous characteristics in terms of traffic pattern, QoS requirements, and possible use of control mechanisms, making it suitable for a given type of resource allocation [25]. The service categories are as follows:

- **Constant bit rate** (CBR): This service category is intended for real-time traffic that requires tightly constrained **cell transfer delay** (CTD) and **cell delay variation** (CDV), and it needs to be handled with a fixed bandwidth. It is characterized by a **peak cell rate** (PCR) value that is continuously available during the connection lifetime of the application. A CBR source may emit cells at or below the PCR any time and for any duration. Examples of

CBR applications are voice and fixed bit rate coded video applications, and circuit emulation services.

- **Real-time variable bit rate** (rt-VBR): This service category is intended for real-time traffic from bursty sources; it can usually tolerate statistical multiplexing with traffic from other sources. It is characterized by the PCR, a **sustainable cell rate** (SCR), and a **maximum burst size** (MBS). Cells which are delayed beyond the values specified by the CTD are assumed to be of significantly less value to the application. An example of rt-VBR application is variable bit rate coded video.

- **Non-real-time variable bit rate** (nrt-VBR): This service category is intended for applications that have bursty traffic and do not have tight constraints on the delay and delay variation. Like the rt-VBR, the traffic parameters are the PCR, SCR, and MBS. It permits statistical multiplexing with traffic from other sources. It expects a low cell loss ratio (CLR) and a bound on the CTD. An example of nrt-VBR application is data.

- **Available bit rate** (ABR): This service category is intended for sources that can adapt to a time-varying available bandwidth; that is, they are able to reduce or increase their information rate if the network requires them to do so. This allows them to exploit the changes in the ATM traffic in the network. They have a specified PCR and are guaranteed a **minimum cell rate** (MCR) which may be zero. Such traffic comes from applications with vague throughput and delay requirements that can only express their data rates in terms of a range of acceptable values. They are subject to a rate-based flow control that uses **resource management** (RM) cells. An example of ABR traffic is LAN emulation traffic.

- **Unspecified bit rate** (UBR) service category is a "best effort" service that is intended for non-critical applications that do not require tightly constrained delay and delay variation nor a specified QoS. It supports statistical multiplexing among sources and does not specify traffic-related service guarantees.

4.6 Summary

ATM traffic has been characterized in different ways, and most of them have been reviewed in this chapter. These include the user service classes, the ATM adaptation layer traffic classes, the QoS classes, and the service category classes. The service category classification attempts to ensure that the ATM layer behavior remains independent of both the ATM adaptation layer protocols and the higher layer protocols. Instead, it relies on the traffic patterns and QoS requirements. Some of the other classifications are based on either the ATM adaptation layer protocols or the higher layer protocols or both.

CHAPTER 5

The ATM Adaptation Layer

5.1 Introduction

The ATM adaptation layer (AAL) gives the ATM network the ability to carry many traffic types. It is not a network process; it is performed at the user's side of the user-network interface (UNI). It segments user packets into 48 bytes of payload that are presented to the ATM layer. The latter adds a 5-byte header to each payload to generate the 53-byte ATM cells. Due to the fact that different applications make different types of demand on the network, the adaptation process is different for the different AAL types. The basic principles of the adaptation process will be presented first, followed by the detailed discussion on the adaptation process that is specific to each AAL type.

5.2 The Adaptation Process

The AAL consists of 2 sublayers [26]: the **convergence sublayer** (CS), and the **segmentation and reassembly sublayer** (SAR). The function of the CS is to divide very long user packets into fixed-length packets called **CS-service data units** (CS-SDUs). It may add header and/or trailer information to the CS-SDU to generate a **CS-protocol data unit** (CS-PDU). Finally, it passes the CS-PDUs to the SAR as SAR-SDUs. (Recall from Chapter 1 that a PDU is a data packet containing user information and control information that is exchanged between two communicating peers in a network. An SDU is a PDU received from the layer directly above the current layer and to which the current layer may add control information to form its own PDU.) Figure 5.1 is a summary of this process.

At the source end, the segmentation and reassembly sublayer is responsible for segmenting each CS-PDU received from the convergence

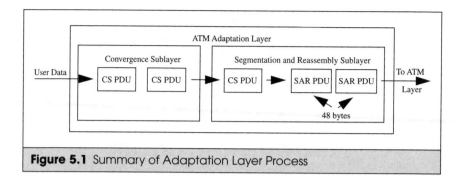

Figure 5.1 Summary of Adaptation Layer Process

sublayer into fixed-length SAR-SDUs according to the application traffic type. The SAR then appends a header and/or trailer to each SAR-SDU to generate an SAR-PDU that it sends to the ATM layer. At the destination, the SAR is responsible for reassembling all SAR PDUs belonging to the same CS-PDU and presenting the reassembled CS-PDU to the convergence sublayer. The detailed AAL process for a generic traffic type is as shown in Figure 5.2.

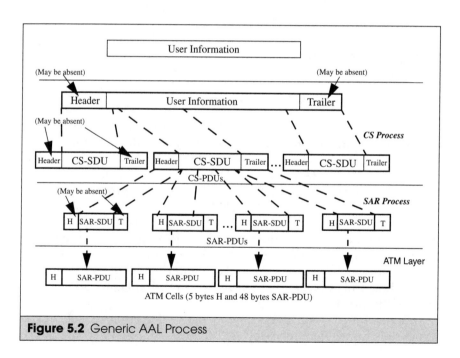

Figure 5.2 Generic AAL Process

5.3 AAL Process for Different AAL Types

The ATM adaptation layer process is different for each ATM adaptation layer type. This section will examine the AAL process for the different ATM adaptation layer types.

5.3.1 AAL Type 1

Constant bit rate (CBR) services use AAL type 1. As discussed in Chapter 4, the CBR service category deals with real-time traffic that requires tightly-constrained cell transfer delay and cell delay variation.

There are two transfer modes for the AAL1: **unstructured data transfer** and **structured data transfer**. In the unstructured data transfer mode, the user data is seen as a continuous bit stream without any internal structure, such as byte-aligned blocks or internal framing bit patterns. This is equivalent to using the T1 channel to transmit only one application. The structured data transfer mode contains information about the internal byte-aligned structure of the user data bit stream. This is also similar to using the T1 channel to transmit more than one application simultaneously in a time-division multiplex manner. Here, information is provided on the beginning and end of each "frame" in the bit stream.

Figure 5.3 shows the AAL process for the unstructured data transfer. In this case, the convergence sublayer adds no header or trailer to

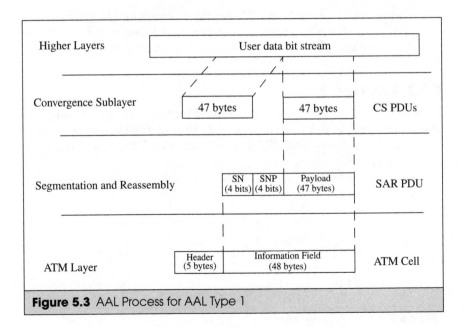

Figure 5.3 AAL Process for AAL Type 1

the user data received from higher layers. It partitions the user data into units of 47 bytes which it passes to the SAR sublayer. The latter appends a 1-byte header to form 48 bytes that it forwards to the ATM layer. At the receiving end, the SAR sublayer receives 48 bytes from the ATM layer and passes the 47 bytes of payload to the convergence sublayer.

In some applications where the structured data transfer is used, one byte of the 47 bytes from the convergence sublayer is used as a pointer that delineates the structure boundaries. The remaining 46 bytes are user data. The pointer denotes the offset, measured in bytes, of the pointer field and the start of the structured block consisting of the remaining 46 bytes of this PDU and the 47 bytes of the next PDU.

The header appended by the SAR contains the following fields:

- A 4-bit sequence number (SN) field used for detecting cell loss or cell misinsertion. SN is divided into two subfields: a 1-bit convergence sublayer indicator (CSI) and a 3-bit sequence count. The CSI bit is used to indicate the existence of an 8-bit pointer field as described above. CSI = 1 if the pointer is present, and CSI = 0 otherwise.

- A 4-bit sequence number protection (SNP) field used to provide error detection and error correction capabilities for the SN field. It consists two subfields: a 3-bit cyclic redundancy check (CRC) field and a 1-bit parity bit. These allow it to correct all 1-bit errors and to detect all 2-bit errors.

The structure of the SAR PDU header is illustrated in Figure 5.4.

Figure 5.5 shows an example of a structured data transfer segmentation and reassembly PDU and an unstructured data transfer SAR PDU.

5.3.2 AAL Type 2

Presently, no standards have been defined for this AAL type. It supports connection-oriented VBR services with timing relation between the source and the destination. Timing recovery in a VBR system is a com-

SN		SNP	
CSI	Sequence Count	CRC	Parity
1 bit	3 bits	3 bits	1 bit

Figure 5.4 SAR PDU Header

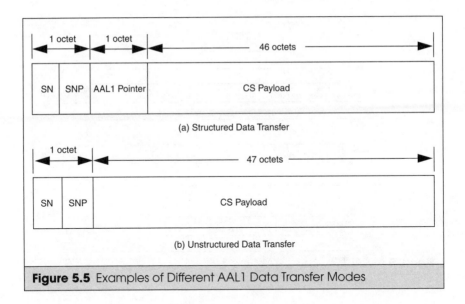

Figure 5.5 Examples of Different AAL1 Data Transfer Modes

plicated process. This is one of the reasons why connection-oriented services use mostly AAL type 1.

5.3.3 AAL Type 3/4

In this type of AAL the convergence sublayer is further divided into two parts: a **common part convergence sublayer** (CPCS) and a **service-specific convergence sublayer** (SSCS). The SSCS may have zero or more protocols defined, depending on the application. The CPCS provides an unguaranteed transport of variable-length frames up to 65,635 bytes. The CPCS functions require a 4-byte header and a 4-byte trailer. Up to 3 bytes of padding may be added to make the resulting CPCS PDU an exact multiple of 4 bytes. The CPCS PDU is divided into one or more 44-byte segments, each of which has a 2-byte header and a 2-byte trailer appended to it to generate a 48-byte payload that is forwarded to the ATM layer. The AAL process is as shown in Figure 5.6.

The fields in the CPCS PDU header and trailer are as follows:

- **CPI** (common part identifier): Used to indicate the counting units used in the BAsize and Length fields of the CPCS PDU. Currently, only CPI = 0 (units = bytes) has been defined.
- **Btag** (beginning tag): Sender puts the same value of Btag as Etag; if Btag is different from Etag, misassembly has occurred (i.e., the CPCS PDU header has not been associated with the CPCS PDU trailer).

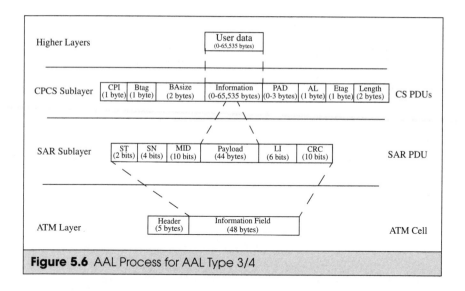

Figure 5.6 AAL Process for AAL Type 3/4

- **BAsize** (buffer allocation size): Indicates the maximum buffering requirement to receive the PDU (>= user data in information field).
- **PAD:** 0–3 bytes of padding are used to make the entire CPCS PDU an exact multiple of 4 bytes.
- **AL** (alignment): A byte of zeros to make the trailer aligned with four bytes.
- **Etag** (end tag): Has the same value as Btag; indicates misassembly if Etag is different from the Btag.
- **Length:** Indicates the number of bytes in the CPCS payload field.

The segmentation and reassembly sublayer PDU header and trailer fields are as follows:

- **ST** (segment type): Used to indicate if the PDU is the beginning of message (BOM), continuation of message (COM), end of message (EOM), or single segment message (SSM).
  - ST = 10: BOM
  - ST = 00: COM
  - ST = 01: EOM
  - ST = 11: SSM
- **SN** (sequence number): Represents the sequence number modulo-16 of each SAR PDU belonging to the same CPCS PDU.
- **MID** (multiplexing identifier): Identifies the CPCS PDU when SAR PDUs from different CPCS PDUs are multiplexed together. The MID value is same for all SAR PDUs belonging to the same CPCS PDU.

- **LI** (length indicator): Length of user data in the payload (in bytes).
- **CRC** (cyclic redundancy check): Used to detect and correct errors.

5.3.4 AAL Type 5

This is a simpler version of the AAL type 3/4. Unlike AAL type 3/4, it does not support multiplexing of data from multiple higher layer applications; as a result, it has no MID field. It allows variable-length frames (up to 65,535 bytes in length) with error detection. The convergence sublayer adds 8 bytes of trailer to the user data. Up to 47 bytes of padding may further be added to allow the resultant PDU to be an integral multiple of 48-byte ATM payloads. The AAL process is illustrated in Figure 5.7, where it is assumed that the SSCS is null. Note that the SAR sublayer adds no header or trailer fields.

The common part convergence sublayer trailer fields are as follows:

- **PAD:** 0-47 bytes which are used to make the CPCS PDU an integral multiple of 48 bytes.
- **UU** (user-to-user indication): Used to transparently transfer one byte of user-to-user information in addition to the user data.
- **CPI** (common part indicator): Used to align the trailer to 64 bits.
- **Length:** Used to indicate the number of bytes of user data in the CPCS PDU payload (i.e., information) field.
- **CRC** (cyclic redundancy check): Used to detect errors in the PDU.

5.4 Signaling AAL

The signaling ATM adaptation layer (SAAL) is the ATM adaptation layer for the control plane. The higher layer protocol for the control

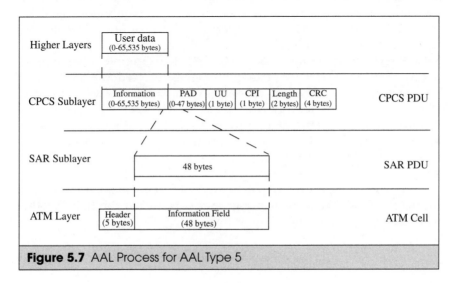

Figure 5.7 AAL Process for AAL Type 5

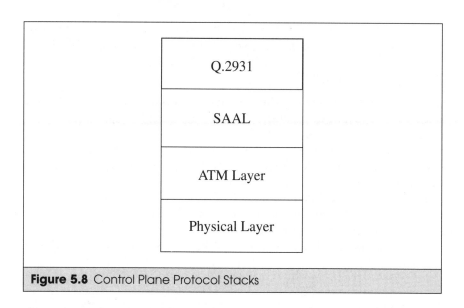

Figure 5.8 Control Plane Protocol Stacks

plane is the access signaling protocol of the ITU-T Recommendation Q.2931 [19]. The SAAL's primary purpose is to provide reliable transport of Q.2931 signaling messages between Q.2931 entities (switches and end systems) over the ATM layer. The control plane protocol stacks are as shown in Figure 5.8.

The SAAL contains two sublayers: a common part (called the **common part AAL,** or CP-AAL) and a **service-specific part**. The latter is subdivided into a Service-Specific Coordination Function (SSCF) and a Service-Specific Connection-Oriented Protocol (SSCOP).

The CP-AAL protocol provides unreliable information transfer and a mechanism for detecting corrupt service data units (SDUs). It uses the AAL5. The SSCOP provides a reliable transfer of signaling information between signaling entities. It also provides a mechanism for the recovery of lost SDUs or SDUs with errors. The SSCF maps the SSCOP services to the needs of the Q.2931. For example, when a user-network interface (UNI) signaling message is received, the SSCF maps the requirements for the UNI message to those of the SSCOP. Similarly, when a network-to-network interface (NNI) signaling message is received, the SSCF maps the requirements of the NNI message to those of the SSCOP. The SSCF in one system does not exchange peer-to-peer messages with the SSCF in another system; it only serves the layers below and above it. This situation is illustrated in Figure 5.9.

As stated previously, SAAL uses the AAL5. The adaptation process is, therefore, similar to that in Figure 5.7. However, the fields in the SDU are slightly different, as shown in Figure 5.10.

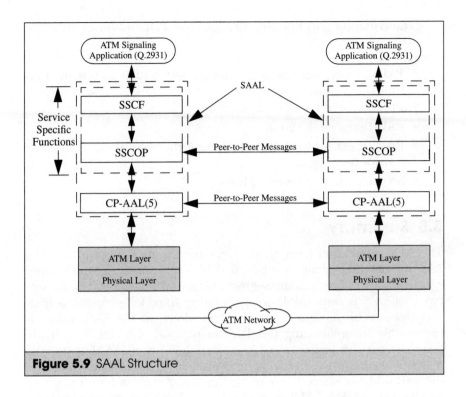

Figure 5.9 SAAL Structure

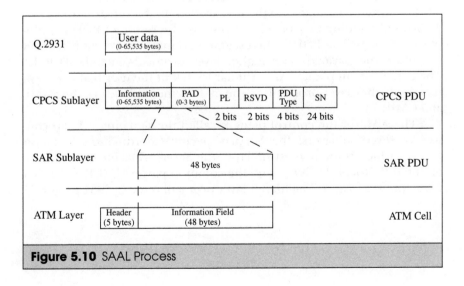

Figure 5.10 SAAL Process

The common part convergence sublayer PDU trailer fields are as follows:

- **PAD:** 0-3 octets are used to make the CPCS PDU an integral multiple of 4 octets.
- **PL** (length of PAD in octets): 2 bits
- **RSVD** (reserved): 2 bits
- **PDU Type:** 4 bits. Used to describe the type of message being transported.
- **SN** (sequence number): 24 bits

5.5 Summary

The ATM adaptation layer (AAL) depends on the type of plane. The AAL for the user plane is subdivided into two sublayers: the convergence sublayer (CS) and the segmentation and reassembly (SAR) sublayer. The CS is responsible for generating fixed-length packets from user application data and passing them down to the SAR, which is responsible for generating the 48-octet payload of a cell. The action taken by the convergence sublayer depends on the AAL type. For AAL1, it segments the user data into units of 47 bytes that it passes to the SAR sublayer where 1 byte of header is added to each unit to generate the payload. For AAL3/4, it adds both a header and a trailer. It may add up to 3 bytes of padding before passing the PDU to the SAR sublayer where the PDU is segmented into units of 44 bytes. 2 bytes of header and 2 bytes of trailer are added to form the payload. For AAL5, 8 bytes of trailer are added to the user data at the CS sublayer and up to 47 bytes of padding may be added to make the resultant PDU a multiple of 48 bytes. The PDU is then segmented into units of 48 bytes that constitute the payload. The higher layer protocols include TCP/IP. The management plane AAL is similar to that of the user plane, except that the higher layer protocols in the management plane are the SNMP and CMIP.

The AAL for the control plane is called the signaling AAL. It consists of three sublayers: the Service-Specific Coordination Function (SSCF), which is the highest sublayer, the Service-Specific Connection-oriented Protocol (SSCOP), and the common part AAL (CP-AAL) that is the lowest sublayer. The higher layer protocol is the Q.2931 protocol.

CHAPTER 6

ATM Network Management

6.1 Introduction

A network is a very complex system. In order for it to provide a level of service that is acceptable to users, it must be properly managed. The term **network management** is used to describe the practice of monitoring and controlling activities in a network to ensure that the level of service a user receives from the network meets the user's needs. It involves the following basic steps. First, management information is gathered, transported, and processed. Then it is stored in a database. At the appropriate time the information is retrieved from the database and used to make decisions that ensure the healthy operation of the network equipment and services.

The existence of many types of networks (local area networks, metropolitan area networks, wide area networks, N-ISDN, B-ISDN, etc.) means that many possible network management models can be defined. In particular, each model can be tailored to meet the needs of a particular type of network. Correspondingly, many types of network management systems need to be developed to handle the different models. This is not an efficient way to solve the complex network management problem.

To avoid this confusion, the ISO has proposed a functional model that classifies network management tasks into five **management functional areas** [27]. These functional areas are: fault management, configuration management, accounting management, performance management, and security management. This is popularly known as the **FCAPS model.**

- **Fault management** is a set of functions that enables the detection, isolation, and correction of problems on the network.

- **Configuration management** provides functions for monitoring the state of network elements and defines procedures for reconfiguring them when changes in their state are detected.
- **Accounting management** provides a set of functions that enables the use of network service to be measured and the costs for such use to be determined. It provides facilities to collect accounting records and set billing parameters for the usage of services.
- **Performance management** provides functions to evaluate and report on the behavior of network elements and the effectiveness of the network or network elements. The role of performance management is to define appropriate performance metrics, gather information on the network, and provide statistical analysis of the information to generate performance data that can be compared with the metrics to evaluate the state of the network.
- **Security management** provides functions that enable network resources to be protected from unauthorized users. Its role is to control access to and use of the network according to the rules established by the network owner.

The network management architecture can be described in terms of three important building blocks: the **network management station,** the **managed object,** and the **management information base (MIB)**. A managed object is a physical device (such as an ATM switch or a router) or logical resource that needs to be monitored and controlled in order to provide an acceptable level of network performance. A MIB is a database which contains information about managed objects.

The network management station is responsible for running the management applications that monitor and control the managed objects. **Management entities** in the network management station are responsible for reacting to **alarms** received from the managed objects. (Section 6.4 will describe alarms.) Management entities are also responsible for polling managed objects to determine the values of some variables.

A managed object is described by four parameters [1]:

- **Attributes** describe the current state and condition of operation of a managed object. An attribute consists of a type and one or more values.
- **Operations** are actions performed on the managed object. These include *create* a managed object and *delete* a managed object.
- **Notifications** are reports provided by the managed object about events that occur within its domain, such as link congestion or link failure.

- **Behavior** is the set of actions exhibited by the managed object in response to operations performed on it. Behavior also includes the object's reaction to the constraints imposed on it, such as reporting on conditions only when their values exceed a predefined threshold.

A managed object runs software that enables it to recognize when predefined attribute thresholds have been reached. This software is called an **agent** and is responsible for sending alarms to the network management station as well as for responding to valid queries from the network management station about information defined in the MIB. Agents are also responsible for storing attribute values in the MIB. Sometimes a managed object contains special agents called **management proxies** which provide management information on behalf of other managed objects.

Generally, a managed object that is represented by a management proxy cannot communicate directly with the network management station because the two entities use different protocols. Consequently, a management proxy acts as a gateway between the managed object and the network management station. The proxy uses the managed object's protocol (which is usually proprietary) to communicate with it and communicates with the network management station using a standard network management protocol.

The MIB identifies the attributes of the managed objects. A network management station monitors network resources (or managed objects) by reading the values in the MIB. Similarly, the resources are controlled by modifying the values in the MIB. Figure 6.1 shows the relationships of the network management building blocks.

The structure of a MIB is usually defined in conjunction with a network management protocol for accessing information in the MIB. The two most commonly used protocols are the **Simple Network Management Protocol** (SNMP) [28] and the **Common Management Information Protocol** (CMIP) [29]. SNMP is designed primarily for TCP/IP networks while the CMIP is designed for the OSI network. SNMP is the more popular of the two protocols; an overview of this protocol will be presented later in this chapter.

Several standards have been developed for managing the ATM network by both the ITU and the ATM Forum. Because the ITU-T **Telecommunications Management Network** (TMN) [30] is designed to accommodate the management of diverse technologies, these ATM network management standards attempt to align with TMN specifications. Before reviewing these standards, it is therefore necessary for us to present an overview of the TMN.

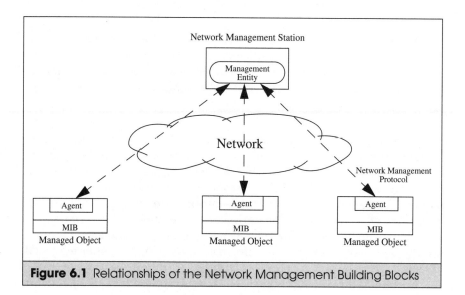

Figure 6.1 Relationships of the Network Management Building Blocks

6.2 Overview of the TMN

TMN is a network of management systems in which each management system manages a part of the telecommunication network and exchanges management information with other systems in the TMN. The basic philosophy of TMN is the separation of the managed telecommunication network from the network that transports management information. TMN uses a separate **data communication network** (DCN) to transfer management information in a manner similar to the Signaling System Number 7 (SS7) network.

An example of the relationship between TMN and the telecommunication network is shown in Figure 6.2 where three telephone exchanges are connected in tandem. From network management point of view, the telecommunication network consists of five managed devices: three exchanges and two transmission systems, where the transmission systems represent the two links between the exchanges. Figure 6.2 shows each of the managed devices connected to the data communication network. Two network management stations which manage different parts of the telecommunication network are also shown connected to the data communication network. A more detailed diagram that shows all the functional components of TMN is presented later in this chapter.

Three architectural views of the TMN are defined, namely information architecture, functional architecture, and physical architecture.

The information architecture refers to the way in which network resources are represented as data structures in managed systems that are observed, modified, and controlled by managing systems via a

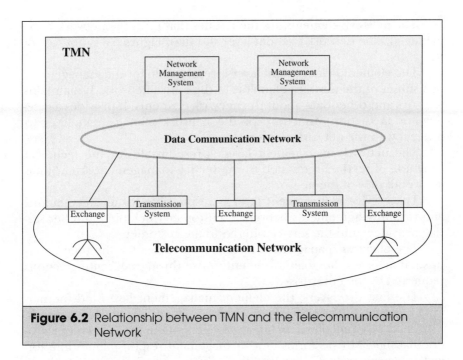

Figure 6.2 Relationship between TMN and the Telecommunication Network

management-agent relationship. TMN uses a logical layered architecture as shown in Figure 6.3. There are four layers: the element management layer, the network management layer, the service management layer, and the business management layer.

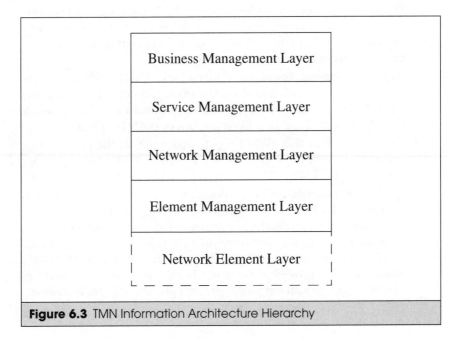

Figure 6.3 TMN Information Architecture Hierarchy

The **network elements** are the entities that form the network to be managed. The network element layer shown in Figure 6.3 is not part of the TMN.

The **element management layer** is responsible for the management of a subset of the network elements in the entire network. It maintains statistics and other data about the network elements. It provides a gateway (or mediation) function for the network management layer to interact with the network elements.

The **network management layer** is responsible for the technical provision of services requested by the service management layer. It has an overall view of the network.

The **service management layer** is responsible for all negotiations and resulting agreements between a customer (including another service provider) and the service offered to the customer.

The **business management layer** is responsible for the total enterprise. It achieves the goals of the enterprise through executing actions requested by the enterprise.

The first two layers, the element management layer and the network management layer, relate to the management of a physical network.

The TMN **functional architecture** refers to the breakdown of activities that the TMN performs in its management responsibilities into formal categories called **function blocks**. There are five function blocks that provide the general capabilities of operations, administration, maintenance, and provisioning within TMN. The five TMN function blocks are as follows:

- **Operations systems function** (OSF) block, which provides overall management responsibilities for the entire TMN. It processes information related to telecommunications management to support various management functions.
- **Network element function** (NEF) block, which communicates with the TMN in order to allow the managed network to be managed. It is responsible for representing the managed functions in the TMN since these functions are not part of the TMN.
- **Workstation function** (WSF) block, which acts as the interface to the human user. Because of this, part of the WSF block operates outside of the TMN.
- **Q-adapter function** (QAF) block, which acts as a converter between TMN functions and non-TMN functions that are similar to NEF and OSF. It translates between a TMN reference point (see definition later in this section) and a proprietary reference point. In effect, it provides an "NEF-like" interface for non-TMN elements. The QAF block is particularly important in the transition to TMN since not all network elements provide a TMN interface.

- **Mediation function** (MF) block, which acts as a converter between an OSF and an NEF (or between an OSF and a QAF or between an OSF and a WSF) in the event that these function blocks have some differences that need to be resolved. The MF block may store, adapt, filter, determine thresholds, and condense information from the NEF. It presents information of a more limited scope to the OSF.

At the service boundaries of the TMN function blocks are **TMN reference points,** which are conceptual points of information exchange between non-overlapping function blocks. In TMN, reference points are indicated with a lower case letter. Three classes of reference points are defined. These are:

- **f-class reference points** are found where a WSF block "attaches" to the TMN (it is usually an X-window interface). The f reference point defines the interface between a WSF and an OSF or an MF.
- **q-class reference points** are found between OSF, QAF, MF, and NEF. There are two classes of q reference points: the q_3 and the q_x. The q_3 defines the interface (or point of information exchange) between the OSF and the QAF, the MF, the NEF, and other OSF within the same TMN. The q_x defines the interface between the MF and the QAF, the NEF, and other MF. The distinction between the two types of reference points lies in the information exchanged across the interface: information exchanged across a q_x reference point requires some conversion before it can be presented to the OSF, while information exchanged across a q_3 reference point does not.
- **x-class reference points** are found between OSFs of two TMNs. They define the interface between two TMNs and are intended to provide interoperability between network providers' networks.

Finally, two other non-TMN reference points are defined. These are:

- **g-class reference points** are found between the user and a WSF.
- **m-class reference points** are found between a QAF and its non-TMN managed resources.

The mediation function (MF) is contained within the network element management layer while the Q-adapter function (QAF) is a part of the network element layer since the QAF provides conversion for non-TMN network elements.

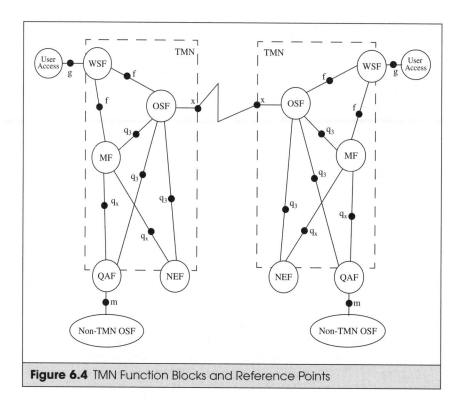

Figure 6.4 TMN Function Blocks and Reference Points

Figure 6.4 illustrates the relationships between the different TMN function blocks and the reference points. In this figure, users access TMN via a device with the WSF functionality. If some conversion is required before the information is presented to the OSF, access is made via the MF; otherwise it is passed directly to the OSF. Similarly, access from a non-TMN network is made via a device that has the QAF functionality. The information may be passed directly to the OSF if no conversion or filtering is necessary; otherwise it is passed to the OSF via the MF where the appropriate processing is done.

Two other important pieces of the TMN are the **data communication function** (DCF), and the **message communication function** (MCF). The DCF provides transport services for information related to telecommunication management between function blocks. These functions include typical functions of the OSI physical, data link, and network layers. The MCF enables the exchange of management information with peer entities. It consists of protocol stacks that allow communication of the functions to the DCF.

The **physical architecture** specifies how the TMN function blocks are mapped into systems and devices in the network, with each function block representing a physical entity (or node). These nodes are:

- **Operations System** (OS): Performs OSFs, but may also provide MFs, QAFs, and WSFs.
- **Mediation Device** (MD): Performs MFs, and may also provide QAFs, OSFs, and WSFs.
- **Q Adapter** (QA): Connects network elements or OSs with non-TMN compatible interfaces.
- **Workstation** (WS): Performs WSFs.
- **Network Element** (NE): Performs NEFs and may provide MFs, QAFs, OSFs, and WSFs.

In addition, the **data communication network** (DCN) provides the data communication function (DCF). DCN implements the transport mechanism used to exchange information between function blocks. Every TMN physical entity may be a TMN element; it may contain additional functionality that permits it to be managed. TMN physical entities are called TMN building blocks. TMN physical interfaces are indicated with an upper case letter. The following interfaces between TMN reference points are defined:

- The **F interface** is between the workstation and the TMN.
- The **Q_3 interface** is between the OS and the TMN building blocks via the DCN.
- The **Q_x interface** is between the MD and the QA and NE via the DCN.
- The **X interface** links TMN building blocks in one TMN with those of another TMN via the DCN.

Figure 6.5 illustrates the TMN physical architecture.

The interfaces Q_3 and Q_x define protocols for connecting transmission systems and equipment to the TMN. While Q_3 is based on the OSI seven-layer model, Q_x is defined at the three lower layers, the physical layer, the data link layer, and the network layer. Also, Q_3 uses the CMIP while Q_x may use any ITU-T recommended protocol. Because of the latitude offered by Q_x, it can be used to support any legacy equipment. In particular, it is suited for ATM network management.

Figure 6.6 shows how the interfaces and reference points are related to the information architecture. Every layer of the information architecture has an operations system function (OSF) that interacts with the OSF in the layer above it and the OSF in the layer below it. The OSF in the Service Management layer of one TMN is responsible for interacting with the OSF in the Service Management layer of another TMN. Also, the interface between the layers in the information architecture is the Q_3 interface; TMN interacts with managed object via the Q_x interface. The ATM management activities are centered on the

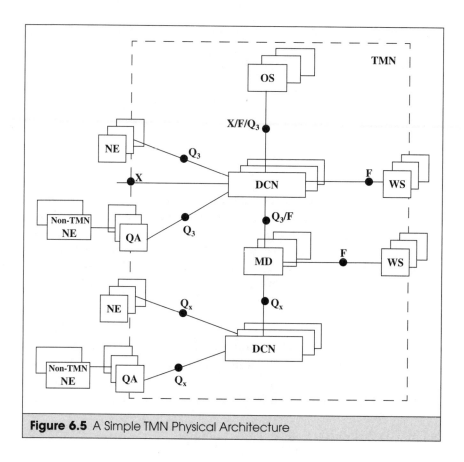

Figure 6.5 A Simple TMN Physical Architecture

Network Management layer, the Element Management layer and the Network Element layer. Finally, note that reference points q_3 and q_x are realized as interfaces Q_3 and Q_x, respectively.

6.3 Overview of the SNMP

As shown in Chapter 1, SNMP is one of the user process protocols in the Internet protocol suite. It uses the User Datagram Protocol (UDP) as the Transport layer protocol. Figure 6.7 shows the SNMP architecture.

As described previously, any network device to be managed by SNMP must contain an SNMP agent. The SNMP agents communicate with the management station through standard messages. There are five types of messages in the first version of SNMP, which is usually referred to as SMNPv1:

- A **GET-REQUEST** message is used by the network management station to retrieve information from a device that has an SNMP agent.

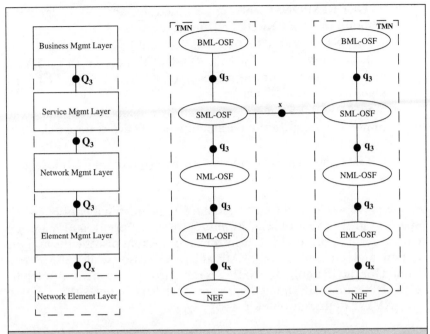

Figure 6.6 Intra-TMN and Inter-TMN Interfaces for Information Architecture

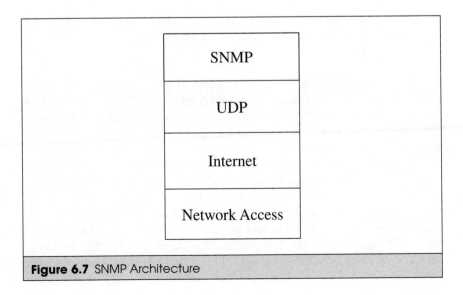

Figure 6.7 SNMP Architecture

- A **GET-RESPONSE** message is used by an SNMP agent to respond to a **GET-REQUEST** message.
- A **GET-NEXT-REQUEST** message is used by a management station as a follow-up to a GET-REQUEST message to retrieve a table of objects. The response to a GET-NEXT-REQUEST message is a Get-Response message.
- A **SET-REQUEST** message is used by a management station to remotely configure the parameters of a network device that has an SNMP agent.
- A **TRAP** message is an unsolicited message that an SNMP agent sends to a management station.

SNMPv2 was introduced to enhance the functionality of SNMPv1, especially in the areas of security, multiprotocol support, and manager-to-manager support. It has security mechanisms that provide the authentication and encryption of SNMP messages. Also, while SNMPv1 is defined for the IP network, SNMPv2 is standardized for the IP, Appletalk, Novell IPX, and OSI Connectionless Network Service networks. SNMPv2 defines two new message types:

- An **INFORM-REQUEST** message permits a network management station to send trap type information to another network management station and request a response, thereby allowing communication between distributed or hierarchical network management systems.
- A **GET-BULK-REQUEST** message permits a network management station to retrieve a large block of information. Unlike the GET-NEXT-REQUEST message which requires the message to be issued for the next item in a table, the GET-BULK-REQUEST message permits a number of items to be requested with one message.

The Internet MIB defines managed objects using a framework called the **structure of management information** (SMI). SMI defines how management information is grouped and named as well as the allowed operations, data types, and syntax for specifying MIBs. A MIB can be depicted as a tree with individual data items making up the leaves of the tree. **Object identifiers** (OIDs), which are organized hierarchically as in telephone numbers, uniquely identify MIB objects in the tree.

The root of the MIB tree has no name or number, but it has the following three branches: International Telecommunication Union - Telecommunication Standardization Sector (labelled ITU-T(0)), International Organization for Standardization (labelled ISO(1)), and joint ISO and ITU-T (labelled Joint ISO/ITU-T(2)). The ISO branch has a few sub-trees, one of which is the Organizations (org(3)) sub-tree. The

US Department of Defense (DOD) is a sub-tree of Organizations and is labelled dod(6). Finally the Internet is a sub-tree of DOD and is labelled Internet(1).

The Internet has four sub-trees: Directory(1), Management(2), Experimental(3), and Private(4). The Directory sub-tree is reserved for future use. The Management sub-tree is intended for DOD protocols and includes the sub-tree MIB(1). The Experimental sub-tree is reserved for the development of experimental MIBs. These MIBs are on standards track and are moved to the Management sub-tree when they have been approved. The Private sub-tree allows vendors to create objects to manage specific entities on their products. This sub-tree has only one branch: Enterprises(1). Each vendor who registers for an enterprise object identifier is assigned a branch in the enterprises sub-tree. For example, Xyplex Networks is assigned the branch number 33. Figure 6.8 shows the MIB tree structure.

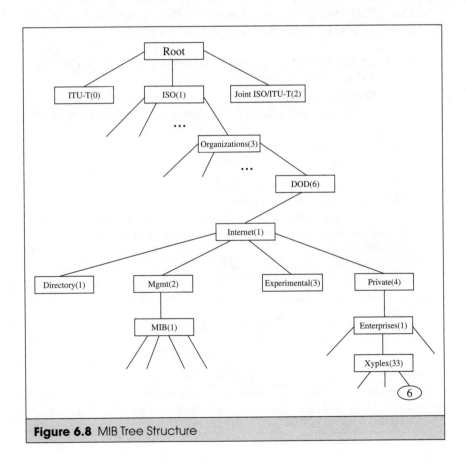

Figure 6.8 MIB Tree Structure

An object's identifier is obtained by explicitly enumerating the nodes that lie on the path from the root of the tree to the node where the object is located. For example, an object located at the node labelled 6 on the Xyplex Networks sub-tree in Figure 6.8 can be reached from the root as follows:

ISO	Org	DOD	Internet	Private	Enterprises	Xyplex	Object
1	3	6	1	4	1	33	6

This object has the OID given by 1.3.6.1.4.1.33.6.

The Internet MIB-II is organized around object groups. These groups include the systems (sys) group, the interfaces (if) group, the transmission (tr) group, the address translation (at) group, the IP (ip) group, the Internet Control Message Protocol (icmp) group, the SNMP group, the TCP group, the UDP group, the Exterior Gateway Protocol (egp) group, the Remote Monitoring (rmon) group, and the Border Gateway Protocol (bgp) group. Figure 6.9 shows the MIB structure.

The SNMP group contains about 30 objects that are used with SNMPv2. These objects fall into five groups as follows:

- The **SNMPv2 statistics** group provides objects that give statistics about this SNMPv2 manager or agent.
- The **SNMPv1 statistics** group provides objects that give statistics about this SNMPv2 manager or agent that communicates with SNMPv1.
- The **object resource** group provides information on the objects that an agent can define dynamically.
- The **trap** group contains a table of information about each of the traps an agent can send.
- The **set** group defines how two or more managers can send SET messages to a single agent in a coordinated manner.

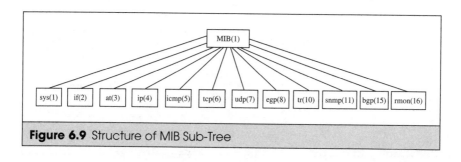

Figure 6.9 Structure of MIB Sub-Tree

Two other MIBs have been defined to help with the management of SNMPv2. These are:

- The **manager-to-manager MIB** contains two groups of objects that provide information about how an SNMPv2 manager (i.e., management station) performs.
- The **party MIB** contains four groups of objects that describe and configure the parties associated with an SNMPv2 entity.

6.4 Operations and Maintenance Cell Flows

Managing an ATM network includes monitoring the network resources, detecting and reporting abnormal behavior of the resources (or the presence of faults and failures), and controlling the resources by taking action to correct abnormal states. These activities, which cover ATM layer management and physical layer management, are aspects of the **operations and maintenance** (OAM) functions specified in ITU-T Recommendation I.610 [31] for the following areas:

1. Performance monitoring through continuous or periodic checking of managed objects leading to generation of maintenance event information.
2. Defect and failure detection through continuous or periodic checking of managed objects leading to the generation of maintenance event information or various alarms.
3. System protection, which involves excluding a failed managed object from operation.
4. Failure or performance information that is given to an appropriate management entity that responds by generating alarm indication and status event report.
5. Fault localization, which is used by internal or external test systems when failure information is insufficient.

These OAM functions are performed on five hierarchical levels associated with the ATM and physical layers. These layers correspond to five bidirectional **OAM flows** labelled F1, F2, ..., F5. The first three are associated with the physical layer while F4 and F5 are associated with the ATM layer and are carried within the ATM cell. F5 flows operate at the virtual channel level and flow between network elements that perform virtual channel connection termination. F4 flows operate at the virtual path level. These flows are illustrated in Figure 6.10 which shows a set of virtual path (VP) switches and one virtual channel (VC) switch in tandem. Recall that a virtual path connection (VPC) extends between two points where the virtual channel identifier (VCI)

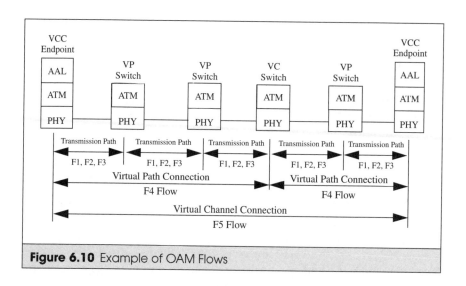

Figure 6.10 Example of OAM Flows

is originated, translated, or terminated. Similarly, a virtual channel connection (VCC) extends between two points where the cell information field is exchanged between the ATM layer and the user of the ATM service.

OAM information is exchanged between ATM entities via the OAM cell. At the ATM layer, OAM cells are specially marked cells which are injected and extracted for a given virtual path or virtual channel connection cell flow. They are identified by an indicator in the ATM cell header. OAM cells for virtual path cell flow are identified by preassigned virtual channel indicator (VCI) while those for virtual channel cell flows are identified by the use of a pre-assigned payload type identifier (PTI).

OAM cells for the F4 flow have the same VPI value as the user (or data) cells of the VPC. Two kinds of F4 flows can exist simultaneously in the same VPC:

- **End-to-end F4 flow** is identified by VCI = 4 and is used for end-to-end VPC operations communication.
- **Segment F4 flow** is identified by VCI = 3 and is used for communicating operations information within the boundaries of one VPC link or multiple inter-connected VPC links where all of the links are under one organization.

Similarly, OAM cells for the F5 flow have the same VPI/VCI values as the user cells of the VCC and are identified by the PTI. Two kinds of F5 flows which can exist simultaneously in a VCC:

- **End-to-end F5 flow** is identified by PTI = 5 and is used for end-to-end VCC communications.

- **Segment F5 flow** is identified by PTI = 4 and is used for communicating operations information within the boundaries of one VCC link or multiple inter-connected VCC Links which are all under the control of one organization.

F4 and F5 flows are terminated only at the endpoints of a VPC (or VCC), but intermediate nodes along the VPC (or VCC) may insert OAM cells. The intermediate nodes may also monitor the OAM cells passing through them.

When a network element such as a switch detects a failure at the physical layer, it generates a physical layer OAM cell carrying the **alarm indication signal** (AIS) alarm. This cell is sent by an ATM network element to its downstream neighbors to allow these network elements to re-establish a virtual channel connection across alternate paths. The network element that detects a fault will send the **remote defect indication** (RDI) back to the source to notify it of the fault on its VCC. On receiving the RDI, the source sends the **far-end receive failure** (FERF) alarm to the destination, notifying it of the fault so that the VCC can be re-established. The ATM Forum specifies only AIS and FERF. In this case, the FERF alarm is sent to the source while AIS is sent to the downstream nodes. Figure 6.11 shows an example of the use of AIS and FERF in fault reporting in the ATM Forum fault management model.

Different actions are taken for different types of failures. For example, in the event of a switch failure, switches adjacent to the failed switch will generate AIS cells that are sent to their downstream neighbors. If only one side of the VCC is affected, a switch will generate an AIS cell that is sent to the source. The latter then sends a FERF cell to the destination so that an alternate connection can be established.

When the physical layer generates an OAM alarm, it informs the ATM layer about the problem. This then triggers an alarm in the ATM layer; F4 and F5 OAM cells are generated to convey AIS/FERF alarms to the appropriate neighbors.

While AIS and FERF are useful in communicating failure information throughout the network, they are not helpful for fault localization. **OAM loopback** cells are used for verifying part of or complete end-to-end connectivity. The loopback can occur within the private network; it

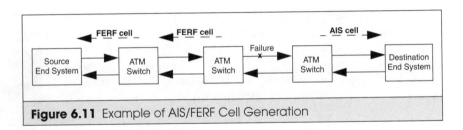

Figure 6.11 Example of AIS/FERF Cell Generation

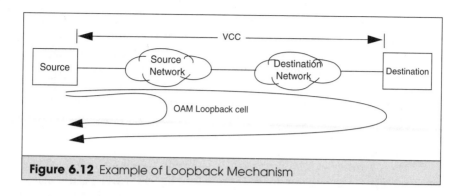

Figure 6.12 Example of Loopback Mechanism

may also occur anywhere outside the private network for virtual channel connections that span two or more ATM network systems. Figure 6.12 shows an example of loopback in a virtual channel connection that traverses two networks.

6.5 ATM Network Management Reference Model

The ATM Forum has developed a network management reference model that can be used for the total management of ATM networks and services. The model identifies five network management interfaces labelled M1, M2, ..., M5 [32, 33, 34]. The specific functions performed in these interfaces are as follows:

- **M1:** Management interface needed to manage an ATM terminal device.
- **M2:** Management interface needed to manage a private ATM network.
- **M3:** Management interface needed to allow a customer to supervise the use of their portion of a public ATM network.
- **M4:** Management interface needed to manage a public ATM network service, including both network element management and service management functions.
- **M5:** Management interface needed for management interaction between two public network providers.

These interfaces are illustrated in Figure 6.13.

From the description of the TMN interfaces, it can be seen that M3 and M5 can be mapped into the x interface. Similarly M1, M2, and M4 can be mapped into the q_x interface if we assume that the appropriate network management systems are SNMP-based. The ATM network management provides the FCAPS functions as well as traffic manage-

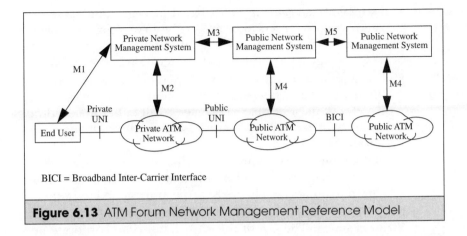

Figure 6.13 ATM Forum Network Management Reference Model

ment. Traffic management is a function that ensures that the quality of service received by a user is exactly (or very close to) that which the user desires. Chapter 7 is devoted to traffic management.

6.5.1 The M1 Interface: ATM Terminal Device Management

Many network management applications and products currently exist for managing network devices such as routers, bridges, and hubs. Their capabilities can easily be extended to manage ATM end systems by incorporating the appropriate MIB object groups. (ATM MIBs are discussed later in this chapter.) Since these network management products are SNMP-based, M1 is essentially an SNMP-based interface.

6.5.2 The M2 Interface: Private ATM Network Management

The M2 interface specifies protocols for managing the private ATM network. Private ATM networks are essentially used to interconnect existing (legacy) local area networks. The operators of these legacy networks typically have in place network management systems that are optimized for managing traditional shared access-based technology. However, ATM is a networking system that has shifted from the shared access-based technology to the switched network technology. As a result, all the network management systems that have been designed for the legacy data communication networks cannot handle the management of the private ATM network.

In addition to the FCAPS and traffic management functions, a management system for a private ATM network must perform other tasks including the following:

- **Policy-based management:** Policy-based management is a service that allows network users to be grouped into workgroups. Policies are defined which specify access privileges that apply to all members of a workgroup regardless of their location in the network.
- **Call management:** Since an ATM network is a connection-oriented network, a network management system for a private ATM network must be able to manage a call rather than individual packets in the call as is the case in connectionless access networks.
- **Virtual circuit provisioning:** It must be able to provision both switched virtual circuits and permanent virtual circuits. It must also permit broadcast channels to be provisioned in either a point-to-multipoint or multipoint-to-multipoint manner.
- **Virtual routing:** The use of the ATM network in corporate networking can reduce dependence on the traditional router in the network. To accomplish this, the network management system must provide **virtual routing** functionality through elaborate directory services that permit any MAC address to be mapped to any network address (including ATM), and vice versa. In this way, the network becomes oblivious to the layer 3 and higher layer protocols, and both routable and non-routable protocols are easily handled.

6.5.3 The M3 Interface: The Customer Network Management

The M3 interface is usually referred to as the **customer network management** (CNM) [32]. It allows a customer to have a direct access to the network management system of the carrier's public network. It also enables the customer to view the carrier's network as a single logical switch and provides two classes of functions:

- **Class 1** is an SNMP-based service that enables a public network provider to provide monitoring information on the configuration, fault, and performance management of a specific customer's portion of a public ATM network. Examples of the services in this class include retrieving performance management data for a UNI link and reporting an alarm message following the loss of a UNI link.
- **Class 2** is also an SNMP-based service that allows the customer to request the addition, modification, or deletion of virtual connections and subscription information in a public ATM network. For example, a customer may request a new ATM virtual path between two of their existing UNI connections to the public network.

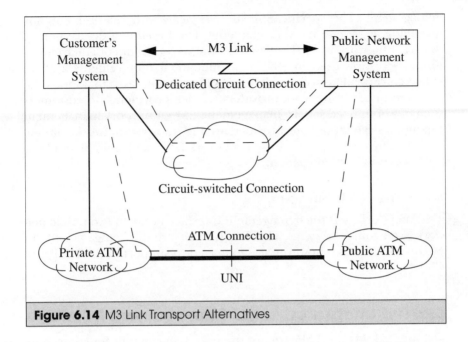

Figure 6.14 M3 Link Transport Alternatives

The link between the customer's network management system and the carrier's network management system can be a private (dedicated) line, a dial-up circuit, or an ATM switched circuit, as shown in Figure 6.14. The choice of the appropriate alternative can be based on a number of factors including cost, security, and reliability. Each M3 interface has a set of managed objects that is sufficient to support M3 functions at the interface. The objects are organized in a standard MIB structure in conformance with the ATM MIB [35].

6.5.4 The M4 Interface

The M4 interface is the management interface for a carrier-based (or public) network. It supports both the CMIP and SNMP and relates to the Q3 interface of the TMN. It interacts with the lower three layers of the TMN model shown in Figure 6.3. Two aspects of the M4 interface have been addressed by the ATM Forum. These are the management of individual ATM network elements (NEs) [33], and the management of aggregates of network elements such as subnetworks [34]. In both [33] and [34], the MIBs for the M4 interface are defined in a protocol-independent manner. However, a CMIP specification for the interface is given in [36].

The following areas of network management are addressed in [33] for managing the individual network elements: configuration management, fault management, performance management, and security management. The specification in [34] deals with requirements for managing aggregate network elements. The functional description of the ATM network in [34] is based on the network functional architecture description used in [37]. The functional requirements are the expected capabilities of the Network Management layer to address the different needs of network providers, service providers and customers each of whom need service management and/or network management capabilities. The functions provided are the transport network configuration management, the transport network fault management, and the network security management.

6.5.5 The M5 Interface

The M5 interface is the management interface between two public network management systems. The details of M5 are still being worked out by the ATM Forum; however, it is expected to support both SNMP and CMIP.

6.6 The Integrated Local Management Interface

M1, M2, M3, M4, and M5 are not the only management functions relevant to the ATM network. The **Integrated Local Management Interface** (ILMI) [38] (formerly called **Interim Local Management Interface**), which has been specified by the ATM Forum, provides an ATM link-specific view of the configuration and fault parameters of a user-network interface (UNI). It is embedded in the UNI and defines how certain basic operations are performed across the UNI. It provides each ATM device (switch or end-system) with status and configuration information concerning the physical interfaces and ATM parameters (virtual path connections and virtual channel connections) available at its interface. Each ATM interface has a set of managed objects, the **ATM interface ILMI attributes,** that is sufficient to support ILMI functions at the interface. The objects are organized in a standard MIB structure, and there is one ILMI MIB structure instance for each ATM interface on each ATM device.

For any ATM device there is an ATM **interface management entity** (IME) associated with each ATM interface that supports ILMI functions for that interface. (IME was formerly called UME, which stands for **UNI management entity.**) When two ILMI-capable ATM devices are connected in a point-to-point manner, ILMI communication takes place between adjacent IMEs and one IME can access the ILMI MIB information associated with the other IME. ILMI is based on a limited subset of the SNMP; specifically, ILMI communication protocol is SNMP/AAL5 (i.e., SNMP without UDP and IP addressing).

Figure 6.15 shows how the IMEs are interconnected.

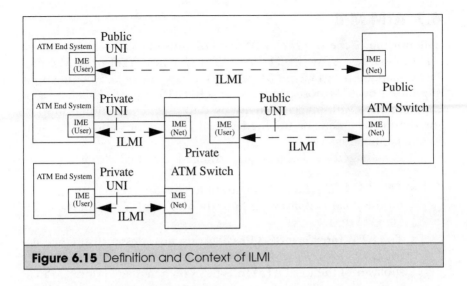

Figure 6.15 Definition and Context of ILMI

Usually both of the adjacent IMEs contain the same MIB but the semantics of some MIB objects may be interpreted differently. ILMI functions also provide for address registration across the UNI. This registration operates as follows: Each UNI has a "user" side and a "network" side. In a UNI between an end system and an ATM network, the end system side is the user side of the UNI, and the ATM switch side is the network side of the UNI. Similarly, in a UNI between a private ATM switch and a public ATM switch, the private ATM side is the user side of the UNI while the public ATM switch side is the network side of the UNI. As shown in Figure 3.5, the ATM address format contains multiple fields including the End System Identifier (ESI) field, which is 6 octets, and the Selector (SEL) field, which is 1 octet. These two fields comprise the **user part** of the ATM address, which is supplied by the end system (i.e., the user side of the UNI). The other fields constitute the **network prefix** of the ATM address, which is supplied by the network side of the UNI. Network prefix usually has the same value for all ATM addresses on the same UNI. The end system communicates with the private ATM switch to which it is physcially connected over the well known VPI/VCI value (0, 16), which is reserved for ILMI. When the ATM switch discovers the end system, it supplies the network prefix to the end system. The latter appends its MAC address to the network prefix to form its complete ATM address. Generally, the value of the SEL field is irrelevant; what matters is only the value of the ESI field.

For LAN emulation, ILMI functions provide for auto-configuration of a LAN emulation client. Finally, they allow an end system's UNI version to be determined when the end system is discovered by the ATM switch.

6.7 ATM MIB

The portion of the Internet MIB that contains objects used to manage ATM interfaces, ATM virtual links, ATM switches, ATM networks, and ATM adaptation layer type 5 (AAL5) entities and AAL5 connections supported by ATM hosts, is defined in RFC 1695 [35]. This has been supplemented with objects that are used to provide additional support for the management of switched virtual connections and permanent virtual connections [40].

The managed ATM objects are arranged into the following groups:

- The **ATM Interface Configuration** group contains information on the ATM cell layer configuration of local ATM interfaces on an ATM device.
- The **ATM Interface DS-3 PLCP** group provides performance statistics of the DS-3 physical layer convergence protocol (PLCP) sublayer of the local ATM interfaces on a managed device. PLCP is the protocol within the transmission convergence sublayer that defines the method by which ATM cells will be formatted for a given transmission facility. DS-3 PLCP sublayer is used to carry ATM cells over DS-3 transmission paths.
- The **ATM Interface TC Sublayer** group provides performance statistics of the transmission convergence (TC) sublayer of the local ATM interfaces on a managed device. A TC sublayer is a sublayer within the physical layer.
- The **ATM Interface Virtual Link Configuration** group is used to create, delete, or modify ATM virtual links in an ATM host, where a virtual link is the entity that makes up a virtual connection.
- The **ATM VP/VC Cross-connect** group is used to create, delete, or modify ATM cross-connects in an ATM switch or ATM network.
- The **AAL5 Connection Performance Statistics** group is used to provide AAL5 performance information for each AAL5 virtual connection that is terminated at the AAL5 entity contained within an ATM switch or host.

As stated earlier, additional ATM managed objects are defined in [40] for switched virtual connections and permanent virtual connections. However, the ILMI MIB is not equivalent to the ATM MIB. The ILMI MIB contains additional functions that do not exist in the ATM MIB. In particular, the ILMI MIB has an address registry function that allows switches to configure network address prefixes in the end systems attached to them. The address registry function also allows such end systems to configure ATM addresses for the ATM interfaces on the switches. The ILMI MIB has a service registry function that allows the addresses of ATM services, such as LAN emulation configuration server, to be located. ILMI MIB groups are as follows:

- The **Physical Layer** group provides information on the attributes of the physical layer at a UNI. (This group is no longer required in UNI versions newer than UNI 3.1 since this information is now available via standard ATM MIBs.)
- The **ATM Layer** group provides configuration information at the ATM layer that relates to the size of the VPI and VCI fields in the ATM cell header, the number of VPCs and permanent VCCs, and maximum number of VPCs and VCCs allowed at this interface.
- The **Virtual Path Connection** group provides configuration information related to the QoS parameters for the VPC local endpoint.
- The **Virtual Channel Connection** group provides configuration information related to the QoS parameters for the VCC local endpoint.
- The **Network Prefix** group provides a mechanism that allows switches to provide the network address prefixes in end systems.
- The **Address** group allows end systems to automatically configure ATM addresses for ATM interfaces on switches.
- The **Service** registry group provides registry for locating ATM network services, such as the LAN emulation configuration server.

Other ATM services, such as LAN emulation and the private network-network interface, have MIB groups associated with them.

6.8 Summary

This chapter described the steps taken to make an ATM network operate in an efficient manner. The ITU-T FCAPS model was presented with the basic components of a network management system. An overview of the TMN, SNMP, operations and maintenance cell flows, the ATM Forum network management reference model, the ILMI, and ATM MIB was presented. ATM network management is still a developing field while the TMN is still maturing. Since the ATM network is a connection-oriented network, in the next few years much of the ATM network management activities will center around the development of protocols that are compatible with the different TMN protocols. A general discussion of network management can be found in [41, 42, 43].

CHAPTER 7

ATM Traffic Management

7.1 Introduction

When a connection is established, the user has some performance expectations that the network needs to meet. Specifically, at connection setup time the user enters into a contract with the network to deliver a defined quality of service (QoS). As defined in Chapter 4, QoS is a set of performance parameters that includes cell loss ratio, cell transfer delay, and cell delay variation. It is the responsibility of the ATM network to ensure that the quality of service, which a user contracts with the network, is what the user actually receives. Traffic management is concerned with the accomplishment of this task, ensuring that users get the desired quality of service. It is achieved through a combination of several control functions, including the following [44]:

- Resource Management
- Connection Admission Control
- Usage Parameter Control (UPC)
- Congestion Control

Before the network enters into a contract with the user, it needs to know the nature of traffic the user is submitting as well as the desired quality of service. The nature of the traffic is defined by a set of traffic parameters called the **traffic descriptor** and the quality of service is specified through a set of QoS parameters. The remainder of this chapter will describe each of these control functions.

91

7.2 Resource Management

Resource management is concerned with the allocation of network resources in order to separate traffic flows according to service characteristics. An important resource management function is **virtual path provisioning**. As defined in Chapter 3, a virtual path is a group of virtual connections between two endpoints. Virtual path provisioning is an important function for the following reasons:

1. Reserving capacity on virtual path connections (VPCs) in anticipation of future virtual channel connections (VCCs) reduces the processing required to establish individual VCCs. A new VCC can be established by making a simple connection control decision at the VPC endpoints without involving connection processing at any transit switch.

2. VPCs permit the logical separation of traffic types requiring different QoS. The VCCs with similar QoS requirements can be grouped in the same VPC.

3. VPCs allow a group of VCCs to be managed and policed more efficiently.

4. VPC allows path routing to be easily changed by modifying routing information at the VPC endpoints.

Other resource management functions include route selection and bandwidth allocation. Various criteria can be used for route selection including:

- The minimum cost routing in which the path with the lowest cost is used, where the cost measure is properly defined.
- Routing based on a designated transit list, which specifies the nodes that need to be on the path, as is used in the private network-network interface (PNNI) routing (discussed in Chapter 8).
- Restricted transit routing, which specifies the nodes to be avoided.

Buffer allocation is a mechanism for allocating the available buffer space at each switch to all the connections in a fair manner. Buffer allocation is an important ATM network function. If a connection is not allocated enough buffer space at any switch on its path, cells belonging to that connection are likely to be discarded when the connection's space is used up. The result is degraded service and hence a violation of the contract. Fair allocation is required to ensure that no one connection receives more degraded service than others. It must be emphasized that some connections have more stringent QoS requirements than others and so may need more buffer allocation than others. This means that while some connections may receive more buffer allocation than others, two connections with similar QoS requirements must receive similar buffer allocation.

7.3 Connection Admission Control

Connection Admission Control (CAC) is responsible for allocating and tracking bandwidth usage per call. In deciding whether or not a connection with certain announced bandwidth requirement and other QoS parameters is to be established, due consideration is given to the impact of the new call on the existing calls. CAC is also responsible for negotiating a new connection request with users in cases where the QoS desired by a user cannot be met. In this case the user will be offered new QoS parameters, which the user may accept or reject.

As stated earlier, when a network accepts a new connection, it is essentially establishing a traffic contract between itself and the user. The contract starts with the user presenting an ATM **traffic descriptor** to the network. ATM traffic descriptor is a generic list of traffic parameters that can be used to characterize the ATM connection. A **source traffic descriptor** is a subset of the ATM traffic descriptor that is used during connection setup to capture the intrinsic traffic characteristics of a requested connection. A **connection traffic descriptor** specifies the traffic characteristics at the UNI and consists of:

- Source traffic descriptor
- Cell delay variation tolerance (CDVT)
- Conformance definition that is used to specify how to determine the conforming cells of the connection

The CDVT can be explained as follows: When several VCs are multiplexed at a switch for transport over a single physical UNI, the output spacing of the cells belonging to one VC will be different from their input spacing. This is due to the fact that cells of a given connection may be delayed while cells from another VC are transmitted by the switch.

Moreover, cells may be delayed while operations and maintenance (OAM) cells are transmitted. (As discussed in Chapter 6, OAM is a group of network management functions that provide network fault indication, performance information, and data and diagnosis functions.) In general, some randomness is introduced in the inter-cell spacings for the cells in one VC by the multiplexing process. Thus, the delay experienced by each cell in a VC at a switch will be different from that experienced by any other cell in the same VC as a result of the multiplexing process. The CBR traffic is not immune to this phenomenon: The multiplexing process usually converts a CBR traffic into a VBR traffic.

The cell transfer delay (CTD) at a switch refers to the time that elapses from the instant a cell arrives at the switch to the instant the last bit of the cell is transmitted by the switch. Cell delay variation (CDV) is the difference between a single observation of the CTD and the mean CTD on the same connection. The network accommodates some CDV by specifying a cell delay variation tolerance parameter of the UPC function that bounds the CDV. CDV is an important parameter for those applications (usually CBR traffic) that are sensitive to delay variations. It is a parameter that is not negotiated; it is set by the switch and is static for the duration of a call.

A traffic contract consists of the following:

- Connection traffic descriptor
- Requested QoS class
- Definition of a compliant connection that the network uses to handle the connection and not the individual cells.

The source traffic descriptors specified for each ATM service category are as follows [44]:

- Constant Bit Rate: peak cell rate (PCR), CDVT
- Variable Bit Rate: PCR, CDVT, sustainable cell rate (SCR), maximum burst size (MBS)
- Available Bit Rate: PCR, CDVT, minimum cell rate (MCR), initial cell rate (ICR), additive increase rate (AIR), rate decrease factor (RDF), number of cells to be transmitted per resource management cell sent (Nrm)
- Unspecified Bit Rate: PCR, CDVT

The additive increase rate (AIR) is an ABR service parameter that controls the rate at which the cell transmission rate increases. The initial cell rate is a parameter that defines the rate in cells/second that a source should transmit initially and after a period of idleness. The rate decrease factor (RDF) is a parameter that controls the decrease in the cell transmission rate.

7.4   Usage Parameter Control

Enforcing traffic contracts at access points is used to allocate resources fairly among different users. When traffic enforcement (or traffic policing) is done at a user-network interface, it is called **usage parameter control**. Usage parameter control (UPC) is a policing mechanism used by the network to ensure that a traffic source conforms to the traffic contract it established with the network when the connection was established. UPC is performed for each virtual channel connection (VCC) according to the set of traffic parameters specified in the traffic contract. The different UPC mechanisms include:

- Generic cell rate algorithm
- Traffic shaping

7.4.1 Generic Cell Rate Algorithm

After the traffic contract has been established between the source and the network, the latter must devise a means to hold the source to the terms of the contract. The generic cell rate algorithm (GCRA) is a mechanism that the source switch uses to enforce the contract on behalf of the network. It involves two parameters: an increment I and a limit L. The algorithm is denoted as GCRA(I, L). Versions of the algorithm include the **virtual scheduling algorithm** and the continuous-state **leaky-bucket algorithm**. In both of these schemes, cells arriving at the first switch in the ATM network are monitored to check whether they comply with the traffic contract parameters or not. Non-conforming cells are either **tagged** or dropped. Cell tagging operates only on cells with the cell loss priority (CLP) bit set to zero (i.e., CLP = 0 cells); their CLP bit is overwritten to 1 when they are found to be non-conforming. Tagged cells are liable to discard when the network becomes congested. (The CLP bit is found in the header of a cell, as described in Chapter 2. Its role is to define cells that may be discarded when the network becomes congested. Such cells have the CLP bit set to 1; that is, they are CLP = 1 cells.)

7.4.1.1 Virtual Scheduling Algorithm

The virtual scheduling algorithm can be explained as follows: Assume that a user is allowed to transmit at the rate of C bits/second. This means that we expect one bit every $1/C$ seconds. Since a cell contains 424 bits (= 53 × 8), this means that the user's contract is for one cell every $T = 424/C$ seconds. If we divide the time axis into intervals of T seconds, we expect no more than one cell within one interval. To make allowance for burstiness in the user's traffic, we define a small window of t seconds, where t << T, so that if the user's cell arrives within a time interval less than T-t seconds after the last conforming cell, then the user is violating the traffic contract and the cell is declared to be a **non-conforming cell**. If a cell arrives after T-t seconds from the time of arrival of the last conforming cell, the user is not violating the contract and that cell is a **conforming cell**. Figure 7.1 shows the operation of this **virtual scheduler**.

In practice, burstiness in the source traffic is accounted for by permitting a fixed number of cells within an interval of T seconds. If, for

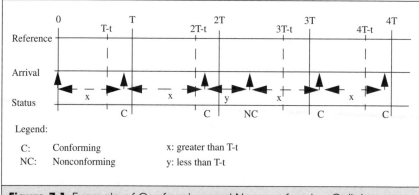

Figure 7.1 Example of Conforming and Non-conforming Cells in a Virtual Scheduler

example, we allow 3 cells in an interval of length T and 4 cells arrive within the interval, the fourth cell will be a non-conforming cell while the first three will be conforming cells. This is illustrated in Figure 7.2 where a maximum of 3 cells may be transmitted in an interval of length T. The length T defines the peak cell rate (PCR = 1/T) while the number of cells allowed in an interval relates to the maximum burst size.

Since the service rate corresponds to the rate to be policed, the virtual scheduling scheme can only be used to enforce one cell rate at a time. For VBR traffic, either the PCR or the SCR can be policed, but not both. Similarly, for ABR traffic, either the PCR or the Allowed Cell Rate (ACR) can be policed, but not both. Two virtual schedulers are normally used back to back in what is called the **dual virtual scheduling scheme**. In the case of VBR traffic, one virtual scheduler can be used to enforce the PCR and the other is used to enforce the SCR. In practice, the virtual scheduler that enforces the PCR essentially controls the cells within a burst and the virtual scheduler that is used to enforce SCR essentially controls the interval between bursts.

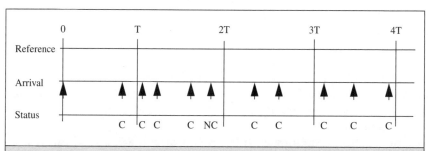

Figure 7.2 An Implementation of the Virtual Scheduling Algorithm

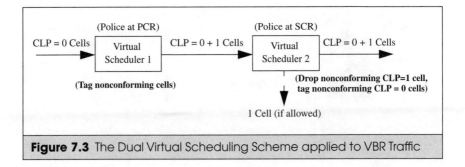

Figure 7.3 The Dual Virtual Scheduling Scheme applied to VBR Traffic

The data stream entering the first virtual scheduler consists of cells with CLP = 0. The first virtual scheduler tags the non-conforming cells, thereby generating a new stream of CLP = 0 + 1 cells that enter the second virtual scheduler. The latter drops the non-conforming CLP = 1 cells (in applications where this is allowed) and tags the non-conforming CLP = 0 cells. This scheme is in Figure 7.3.

7.4.1.2 Continuous-State Leaky-Bucket Algorithm

The continuous-state leaky-bucket algorithm operates in the following manner: A bucket of size B contains tokens that drain at a constant rate R. An arriving cell that finds the bucket's contents to be less than B is defined to be a conforming cell; it then adds a token to the bucket. An arriving cell that finds the bucket full is defined to be non-conforming; it will either be discarded or tagged and sent into the network. A non-conforming cell does not add a token to the bucket. Figure 7.4 shows a schematic of the continuous-state leaky-bucket scheme. The rate R corresponds to the negotiated transmission rate for the source

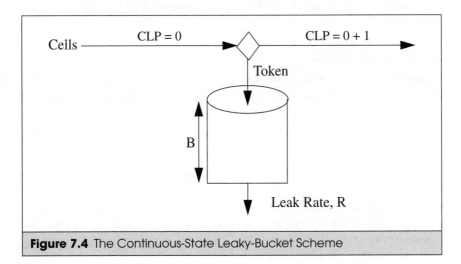

Figure 7.4 The Continuous-State Leaky-Bucket Scheme

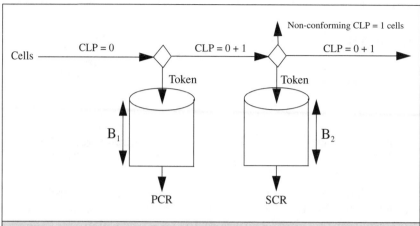

Figure 7.5 The Dual Leaky-Bucket Scheme Applied to VBR Traffic

and the bucket size B represents the maximum burst size that the source is allowed to transmit at the rate R.

As in the virtual scheduling scheme, the dual leaky-bucket scheme [45] can be used to enforce the peak cell rate in the first bucket and the sustainable cell rate (or any other applicable cell rate) in the second bucket. Similar to the dual virtual schedule, non-conforming cells are tagged at the first bucket. If a cell tagged in the first bucket is non-conforming in the second bucket, it is discarded; otherwise it is sent into the network with its tag unchanged. Similarly, if a cell that is conforming in the first bucket is non-conforming in the second bucket, it is tagged and sent into the network. The bucket sizes, B_1 and B_2, are chosen to obtain the desired cell delay variation. The scheme is shown in Figure 7.5.

7.4.2 Traffic Shaping

Most VBR sources go through an on/off cycle in which cells are generated at peak rates during the on period and no cells are generated during the off period. **Traffic shaping** is a mechanism that takes advantage of this cycle to reduce the peak rate by buffering cells before they enter the network and scheduling their entry into the network at a rate less than the peak arrival rate. In this way, the burstiness of the source is reduced and this usually reduces the probability of cell loss in the network. Traffic shaping can also be performed by the network to reduce the peak cell rate or burstiness of VBR traffic by spacing out the cells.

A buffered version of the leaky-bucket algorithm has been proposed for enforcing traffic shaping [46]. In this method, if a cell arrives when the bucket is full, it is buffered until the bucket content decreases by one, at which time it can add its token to the bucket and enter the network. This guarantees that the source never transmits at a rate greater than the leak rate.

7.5 Congestion Control

Despite all the attempts made to prevent network congestion, the network will still become congested from time to time. **Congestion control** is a set of mechanisms that are used to detect the onset of congestion and react to minimize its speed, effects, and duration. Congestion control schemes can be classified into two categories:

- **Preventive congestion control** attempts to prevent congestion by taking appropriate actions before they occur.
- **Reactive congestion control** recognizes that preventive control is usually not enough to eliminate congestion; it is used to recover from a congested state.

Specific techniques used for congestion control include

- Selective cell discarding
- Explicit forward congestion indication

7.5.1 Selective Cell Discarding

Selective cell discarding is a reactive congestion control scheme that is applied by the network to the CLP = 1 cells (i.e., tagged cells) to reduce network congestion. Under this scheme, any switch that experiences congestion will selectively discard some CLP = 1 cells. Congestion may be defined to have set in if the buffer content at a switch exceeds a predefined threshold. Proposals that call for **frame discarding** have also been made; however, the ATM Forum does not recommend this scheme. In frame discarding, a switch that experiences congestion will choose to discard cells belonging to the same connection rather than discarding cells selectively. The method of choosing the frame to discard is arbitrary.

7.5.2 Explicit Forward Congestion Indication (EFCI)

EFCI is a mechanism for communicating congestion information from the network to the user to enable end-to-end control action to be taken. It is essentially a proactive congestion control scheme which is used by a node in an impending congestion state (or already in a congested state) to modify the value of the Explicit Forward Congestion Indication (EFCI) in the payload type (PT) field in the header of the cell, as discussed in Chapter 2. The destination node reads the EFCI bit

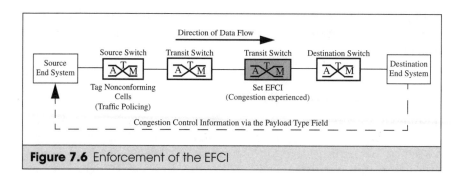

Figure 7.6 Enforcement of the EFCI

and informs the appropriate source to adjust its rate if the bit is set. A node uses a well-defined threshold in its buffer occupancy to determine when to activate the EFCI. When the queue length in its buffer exceeds the threshold, the node activates the EFCI.

EFCI is also a closed-loop congestion control scheme, as illustrated in Figure 7.6. The source switch can tag non-conforming cells (as part of the UPC function) while a transit switch can use the EFCI to indicate a near-congestion state. The destination end system then instructs the source end system to cut back on its rate through the PT field of the cells destined for the source end system.

7.6 ABR Flow Control

As stated above, an ATM network supports constant bit rate (CBR) services, variable bit rate (VBR) services, available bit rate (ABR) services, and unspecified bit rate (UBR) services. Typically, CBR and VBR services are provisioned at the peak cell rate and any remaining bandwidth is used for ABR and UBR services. Except in cases where ABR service is guaranteed a minimum cell rate, ABR and UBR services do not have any guaranteed quality of service.

One of the features of ABR traffic is that the source adapts its rate to the network conditions. Thus, the ATM network will use any slack bandwidth that arises from fluctuations in traffic to transmit more ABR traffic. More importantly, ABR applications must use such available bandwidth almost instantaneously and in such a manner as to ensure that the QoS for the existing CBR and VBR applications are not impaired. For this goal to be achieved, a good flow control scheme is required, one that permits the network to use any temporarily available bandwidth to transmit ABR traffic without adversely impacting the QoS of the CBR and VBR traffic. Two flow control schemes have been proposed for ATM networks. These are the **rate-based** flow control [47], and the **credit-based** flow control [48].

7.6.1 Rate-Based Flow Control

The rate-based flow control scheme is an end-to-end flow control scheme adopted by the ATM Forum. In this scheme, which requires one source and one destination (or one virtual channel) for each feedback loop, the destination alerts the source to slow down its transmission when the network starts to experience congestion. Information about the network status is conveyed to the source through special control cells called **resource management** (RM) cells. A **forward RM** (FRM) cell is sent by the source at regular intervals (after a predefined number of data cells, usually after eight data cells) or under some exception conditions. The FRM cell contains the **current cell rate** (CCR) at which the source is transmitting. It also has a field for the **explicit cell rate** (ER). ER is the rate that a switch on the path through which a VC passes will allow the source to transmit. Any switch that receives an FRM cell may set the EFCI bit but not the ER. When the FRM cell reaches the destination, it is turned around to become a **backward RM** (BRM) cell. When a switch receives a BRM cell, it may insert the ER it can support. If a smaller ER has already been inserted by a downstream switch, the current switch does nothing to the BRM cell. When the BRM cell arrives at the source, the source is expected to set its new CCR to the ER, provided that the ER is not less than the minimum cell rate (MCR).

In addition to the **EFCI marking** of data cells and **ER marking** of RM cells, there is another way in which congestion control can be done in the ATM network. It is called **relative rate marking,** and it works in the following manner. One of the fields of the RM cell is a 1-bit field called the **congestion indication** (CI) bit. It is used to force the source to decrease its **allowed cell rate** (ACR) using a predefined algorithm. The source sets the CI bit to CI = 0 when it sends the RM cell. The destination sets CI = 1 in the BRM cell to indicate that EFCI = 1 was received in a previous data cell. If the congestion indication bit is set (i.e., CI = 1), the source must decrease its ACR by a well-defined proportion of its current value, but the ACR must never be less than the MCR.

Another field in the RM cell is a 1-bit **no increase** (NI) field. It is used to prevent the source from increasing its ACR. Unlike CI = 1, NI =1 does not require any decrease in the ACR. It is typically used when a switch senses impending congestion. It informs the source to observe the CI and ER fields in the RM cell and not to increase its ACR above its current value. Thus, relative rate marking involves setting the NI and CI bits in the RM cell. These markings define two classes of ATM switches:

- **ER switch:** One that can set the explicit rate it can support in the RM cell.

- **EFCI switch:** One that enforces flow control by setting the EFCI bit in the data cell. This switch is also called a **binary ATM switch**. EFCI switches do not understand the contents of the RM cell and pass it transparently.

There is also the possibility of a hybrid switch that uses both schemes. One of the attractive features of the rate-based flow control scheme is that it makes minimal demand on the switches [49]. Specifically, only the edge switches are required to remember state information such as the allowed cell rate for each virtual channel and the new rate that applies to that VC. Switches that are in the interior of the network (i.e., the transit switches) are not required to save any state information.

7.6.2 Credit-Based Flow Control

The credit-based flow control scheme is based on a different control paradigm from the rate-based scheme. It is a hop-by-hop (or link-by-link) flow control that operates in the following manner: The receiving end of each link reserves a certain number of buffers for each virtual channel [50]. (It is estimated that one RTT worth of cell buffers is required for each virtual channel.) The receiving end of a link issues "credits" to the transmitting end. The credits indicate the number of cells that the transmitting end is allowed to send. When this number of cells has been transmitted for the given virtual channel, the transmitting end cannot send any more cells on that VC until new credits are received from the receiving end of the link.

The receiving end cannot send any new credits unless there is enough buffer space at that end to accommodate the transmission. Thus, it maintains a credit balance for each virtual channel; it keeps track of the number of empty buffers outstanding for each VC. When a new cell arrives for a given VC, the receiving end decrements the credit balance by one. Similarly, when the receiving end forwards one cell to the receiving end of its downstream link, it increments the credit balance for that VC by one. Thus, for a given virtual channel, each link maintains its own control loop independent of the other links on the virtual channel connection.

Figure 7.7 shows a comparison of the operation of the rate-based scheme and the credit-based scheme. As the figure illustrates, the forward resource management cell of the rate-based scheme is essentially a request for a new transmission rate. The backward resource management cell specifies the rate that the network can support, which is a form of credit. Thus, the distinction between the two schemes becomes the length of the flow control loop: link-by-link versus end-to-end.

7.6.3 Comparison of the Flow Control Schemes

In the rate-based scheme, only the edge switches need to keep state information. Consequently, only a few switches need to have the

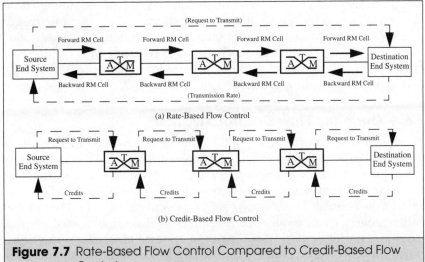

Figure 7.7 Rate-Based Flow Control Compared to Credit-Based Flow Control

specialized functionality of an edge switch, where an edge switch is one through which users' data enters the network. However, as specified in [44], there are thirteen explicit rules for the source behavior, six rules for the destination, and at least twelve parameters to be controlled by the source switch for each virtual channel. This works well if the number of virtual channels is small. However, when the number of virtual channels is large, a lot of bookkeeping is required with an equally high memory requirement.

The rate-based flow control scheme does not ensure that cells are not discarded. Since higher layers like TCP retransmit an entire frame if an error occurs (such as that resulting from discarding a cell belonging to the frame), the loss of one cell can drastically reduce the throughput of the affected virtual channel.

The rate-based scheme reacts very slowly to network congestion. As an end-to-end flow control scheme, its effect often comes too late, especially in networks that have large round-trip time (RTT). (RTT is the time it takes a resource management cell to go from the source to the destination, as a forward RM cell, and back to the source, as a backward RM cell.) This means that the impact of the rate-based flow control scheme is usually felt after congestion is over.

The credit-based scheme uses the so-called **per-VC queueing**. Per-VC queueing requires each switch to maintain a queue for each virtual channel. This implies that each switch must be equipped to track the credit balance for each virtual channel that is supported by the switch. However, credit-based flow control has some advantages over rate-based flow control. One advantage is the fact that it ensures that no cells are lost by granting credits only when there is no risk of buffer overflow. Also, because it uses hop-by-hop instead of end-to-end flow control, it reacts faster to network conditions than the rate-based scheme. In particular, it permits temporarily unused bandwidth allocated to CBR and VBR traffic to be used to transmit ABR traffic. The credit-based scheme also supports the point-to-multipoint topology that makes multicasting possible.

7.6.4 Quantum Flow Control Alliance

The Quantum Flow Control (QFC) Alliance was formed in 1995 after the ATM Forum adopted rate-based flow control. Its goal is to develop a version of credit-based flow control for ABR traffic that overcomes the concerns that have been expressed about the viability of credit-based flow control. It has issued a QFC specification [51]. One major enhancement that the alliance has made to the original credit-based scheme is the definition of two types of credit: **link credits** and **virtual channel (VC) credits**. Link credits are used to ensure that the destination end's buffers do not overflow while the VC credits are used to ensure that no one VC or group of VCs monopolizes the buffer spaces when congestion occurs somewhere downstream.

7.7 Summary

Traffic management ensures that the network operates at such a level that it can meet all the QoS it has contracted with the users. It accomplishes this through a combination of functions including resource management, call admission control, usage parameter control, and congestion control. The ATM Forum has issued a specification for a rate-based flow control of the ABR traffic. An alternative flow control scheme, called credit-based flow control, is the basis for work being done by the Quantum Flow Control Alliance.

CHAPTER 8

Private Network-Network Interface

8.1 Introduction

The user-network interface (UNI) protocols enable an end system to establish connections with other end systems through the ATM network. Similarly the ATM private network-network interface (PNNI) protocols are used to route ATM signaling requests between switching systems. A switching system can be a single switch or a network of multiple switches, all of which are under a single control system. In the absence of any standardized method of interswitching system communication, the only way for communication across switches from different vendors is via permanent virtual circuits (PVCs). Configuring PVCs between every pair of switching systems is burdensome.

To alleviate this problem, the ATM Forum has issued two sets of specifications on PNNI, both of which are designed to support switched virtual circuits (SVCs). The first set was for the Interim Interswitch Signaling Protocol (IISP) [52] (usually referred to as PNNI Version 0). As the name implies, IISP is intended to be used on a temporary basis pending the release of the PNNI Version 1.0 [53], which is the second set of specifications that the ATM Forum has also issued.

This chapter will review the two sets of specifications. However, a greater emphasis is placed on PNNI Version 1.0 since it is expected to eventually replace the IISP.

8.2 IISP

The IISP is designed to support UNI 3.1 with optional support for UNI 3.0. It is not as sophisticated as the PNNI Version 1.0. Figure 8.1 illustrates the IISP reference model. As this figure illustrates, IISP specifies the interface between two switching systems. Two types of

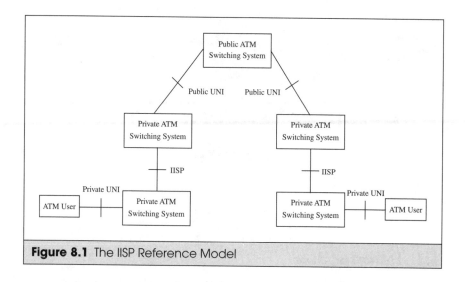

Figure 8.1 The IISP Reference Model

protocols are defined for the interface: **signaling protocols** and **routing protocols**.

IISP supports the use of PVCs which are manually configured. SVCs are established via IISP signaling. In IISP signaling, one switching system on a specific link plays the role of the user side and the other side plays the role of network side, as specified in UNI 3.1. These roles are assigned manually. By convention, the calling party's switching system is the user side and the called party's switching system is the network side of the signaling. At each hop along the path to the destination system, the call setup procedure consults the intermediate switching system's next hop table to see if an entry in the table matches the destination address. If there is no match, the switching system generates a RELEASE COMPLETE message with an indication that there is no route to the destination. If there is a match, the routing function in the switching system identifies the interface in the system for forwarding the call to the destination. If this interface is available to handle the call, the setup message is forwarded to the next switching system on the path to the destination. Otherwise, it returns a RELEASE COMPLETE message with the indication that the network is out of order.

In IISP routing, there is no exchange of routing information between switching systems. It uses a fixed routing algorithm to do hop-by-hop routing after the call setup message has determined the best path based on the next hop tables, as discussed previously.

8.3 PNNI Version 1.0

The ATM Forum PNNI Version 1.0 specifications [53] define two categories of protocols for use between switching systems:

1. The PNNI routing protocol is used to distribute topology information between switching systems.
2. The PNNI signaling protocol establishes point-to-point (or point-to-multipoint) connections across an ATM network.

PNNI Version 1.0 has been designed to support all UNI 3.1 capabilities and some UNI 4.0 capabilities. It is scalable to very large networks, and supports **QoS-based routing,** where QoS-based routing is a routing algorithm that ensures that routes which meet the QoS requirements are selected for each connection. PNNI's dynamic routing protocol enables it to route around failed links and links with insufficient resources. The key to the scalability of the PNNI is the hierarchical organization of the network with summarization of reachability information between levels in the hierarchy. At each level in the hierarchy, PNNI defines a uniform network model that explains how the level operates and how the nodes at that level interact with those in the levels below and above it. Note that IISP implementations will not be interoperable with PNNI Version 1.0 since IISP uses only UNI signaling and not network-network signaling.

8.3.1 Routing Architecture

PNNI views the network as a collection of **peer groups**. At the lowest level, peer groups are formed as collections of switches. All the nodes in a peer group have complete state information on each other, and each peer group is identified by a peer group ID.

Peer groups are in turn organized hierarchically into higher levels of peer groups which are parent peer groups of the lower level peer groups. Within its parent peer group, each peer group is represented by a single logical entity called the **logical group node** (LGN) which acts as a normal node in the parent peer group. The following subsections describe the major PNNI routing functions.

8.3.1.1 Peer Group Leader Election

Each peer group uses a well-defined algorithm to elect its **peer group leader** (PGL). Sometimes preference for the PGL is established through configuration. The PGL for a peer group represents that peer group at the next level of the hierarchy. In addition, the PGL is responsible for executing the functions of the LGN in the next hierarchical level.

8.3.1.2 Hello Protocol

Logical group nodes exchange hello packets to discover and verify the identity of their neighbors. It is through the hello message that the version of the PNNI that an LGN supports is identified. Also, through the hello message a pair of neighboring LGNs can discover whether they are in the same peer group or not. An LGN that is adjacent to another LGN that is in another peer group is called a **border node**. Logical links between nodes in the same peer group are called **horizontal links** or **inside links,** and logical links between nodes in different peer groups are called **outside links**.

8.3.1.3 Topology State Database Exchange

This is a mechanism by which the nodes in a peer group synchronize their topology databases. The topology database includes **topology state information** (a node's characteristics and link state parameters) and **reachability information** (addresses and address prefixes that describe destinations to which calls can be routed). This information is bundled in PNNI **topology state elements** that are flooded throughout the peer group.

8.3.1.4 Topology State Summarization

Topology state summarization permits the amount of information describing a peer group to be reduced as the information goes up the routing hierarchy. The aggregation process is as follows: A child peer group is represented by a logical group node in the parent peer group through the process of **nodal aggregation**. Similarly, a set of links between two peer groups can be represented by a single logical link through the process of **link aggregation**. Finally, ATM addresses that are reachable from a peer group can be represented by a single address prefix. In this way, higher level entities in the hierarchy see only a summary of the state of the lower level entities.

8.3.1.5 Hierarchical Path Determination

PNNI uses source routing for connection setup. The node through which a peer group is entered (the ingress node of the peer group) is responsible for selecting the entire path across that peer group. The path is encoded as a **designated transit list** (DTL) that specifies each node used in transit across the peer group. If a node along the path is unable to follow the DTL for a connection setup request due to lack of resources, the node refuses the request and must **crankback** the request to the node that created the DTL. The crankback procedure is described later in this chapter.

8.3.2 Signaling Architecture

Signaling is used for call/connection establishment and clearing. PNNI signaling uses a subset of the UNI 4.0 signaling. It uses information gathered by PNNI routing; specifically, it uses route calculations derived from reachability, connectivity, and resource information that is dynamically maintained by PNNI routing. The following subsections describe the major PNNI signaling functions.

8.3.2.1 DTL Processing

As stated earlier, a designated transit list (DTL) is a complete path across a peer group that is provided by the source node or an entry border node at a peer group. A hierarchically complete source route is expressed as a sequence of DTLs ordered from lowest to highest peer group level and is organized as a stack with the DTL at the top of the stack corresponding to the lowest level peer group. The stack changes as the call is progressed.

8.3.2.2 Crankback and Rerouting

When a call arrives at a node that does not have the resources to service the call, the switch cranks the call back to the node that created the designated transit list. **Crankback** is a mechanism that allows a connection that is blocked along a selected path to be rolled back to a node earlier in the path and eventually to the node that created the designated transit list from where another path to the destination can be chosen (i.e., from where another designated transit list can be created) which avoids the blocked node or link.

8.4 A Sample PNNI Version 1.0 Network Hierarchy Model

Figure 8.2 is a model used to illustrate the concepts that have been discussed above. In this figure, twelve switches (or nodes), labelled 1 through 12, are shown. Nodes 1–4 are in peer group A (PG(A)), nodes 5–7 are in the peer group B (PG(B)), nodes 8–10 are in the peer group C.1 (PG(C.1)), and nodes 11 and 12 are in the peer group C.2 (PG(C.2)). The hierarchical addresses of the nodes based on their peer groups are also shown. Nodes 2, 6, 10, and 12 are the peer group leaders (PGLs) of their respective peer groups.

Figure 8.3 shows the network abstraction at different levels in the PNNI hierarchy. The figure shows how PG(C.1) and PG(C.2) have been abstracted to form the peer group PG(C) (i.e., LGN C) with the logical node C.1 as the peer group leader. The three logical nodes A, B, and C form the highest level peer group with logical group node B as the peer group leader. Note that the PGL functions for this level are implemented in node 6 (B.2), since it executes the LGN functions and the PGL functions for its peer group. Similarly, the PGL functions for LGN C are implemented in node 10 (C.1.3).

As an example of the use of the crankback mechanism, consider an end system A.1.1, attached to switch A.1, which wants to establish a

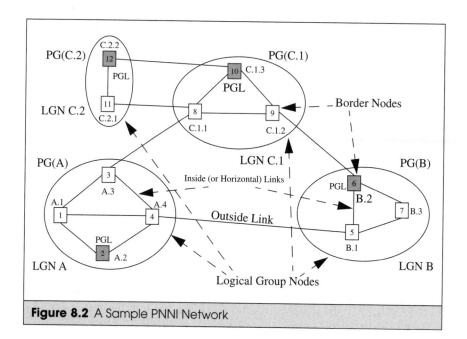

Figure 8.2 A Sample PNNI Network

connection with end system B.3.4, attached to switch B.3. To simplify the discussion, consider the information flow associated with a UNI SETUP message from A.1.1 to A.1. On receiving the message, A.1 constructs the necessary DTLs. There are four possible paths to B.3: (A.1, A.3, C, B), (A.1, A.3, A.4, B), (A.1, A.4, B), and (A.1, A.2, A.4, B). Assume that based on cost and policy, the path (A.1, A.4, B) is chosen. Consider three scenarios:

- **Scenario 1:** The SETUP message is successfully received by B.3 through A.4. The details of this scenario are as follows: On receiving the message, A.4 observes that the next address is B. Since it is adjacent to B though B.1, it forwards the message to B.1 which forwards it to B.3. Here, B.1 is responsible for constructing the detailed DTL for the LGN B. *Note that our presentation has been simplified for the purpose of clarity.* Usually more than one DTL is defined, one for each level of the hierarchy. Each DTL, which specifies a route within one peer group, is organized as a stack with a **current transit pointer** that indicates which element in the list is currently being visited at that level. Figure 8.4 illustrates the information flow for this scenario.

- **Scenario 2:** The link (A.4, B.1) is congested, so when A.4 receives the SETUP message, it returns a RELEASE COMPLETE message that indicates path failure. A.4 initiates the crankback procedure. This prompts A.1 to try another path that excludes

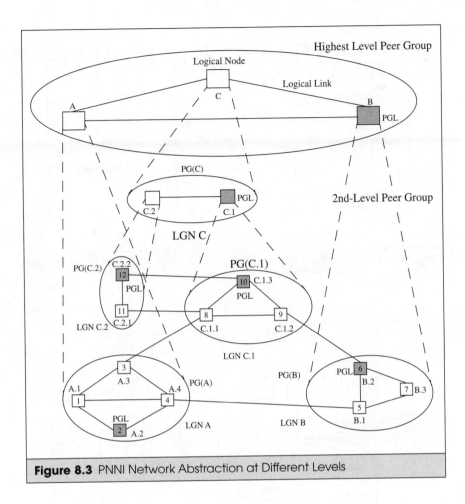

Figure 8.3 PNNI Network Abstraction at Different Levels

A.4 through which the SETUP message can successfully reach B.3. The only path that meets this condition is (A.1, A.3, C, B). Thus, A.1 constructs the appropriate designated transit lists.

A.1 sends the SETUP message to A.3 which observes that its neighbor, C.1.1, is in peer group C. It sends the message to C.1.1. The latter builds a route to B through C.1.2. When C.1.2 receives the message, it notices that its neighbor B.2 is in peer group B. It then forwards the message to B.2 which constructs a route to B.3. The details are illustrated in Figure 8.5.

- **Scenario 3:** The path through A.4 fails and a new path (A.1, A.3, C, B) is selected. However, the link (C.1.2, B.2) is congested and the path also fails. The sequence of activities is as in Scenario 2 except that another crankback procedure is initiated by C.1.2. The details of this scenario are shown in Figure 8.6.

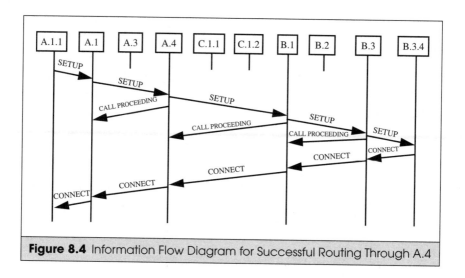

Figure 8.4 Information Flow Diagram for Successful Routing Through A.4

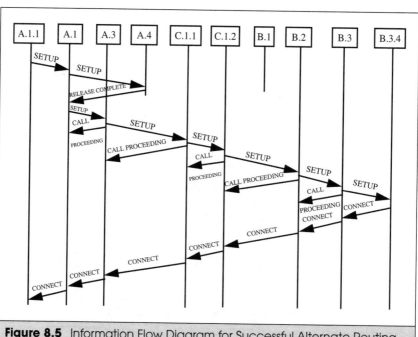

Figure 8.5 Information Flow Diagram for Successful Alternate Routing Through Peer Group C

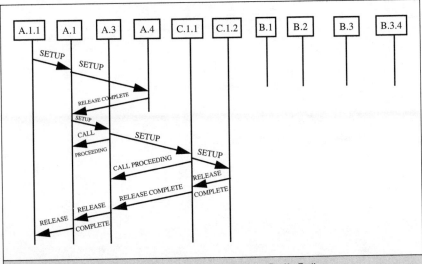

Figure 8.6 Information Flow Diagram for Two Path Failures

8.5 Summary

This chapter discussed how the PNNI routes ATM signaling requests between switching systems. PNNI is intended to provide a method for interoperability of switches from different vendors. The ATM Forum PNNI Version 1.0 specifies two sets of protocols: routing and signaling protocols. The PNNI Version 1.0 is a sophisticated service that replaces the earlier version called the Interim Inter-switch Signaling Protocol (IISP) which is based on UNI signaling 3.1. IISP uses a fixed routing algorithm with static routes. The PNNI Version 1.0 routing protocol views the world as a collection of peer groups with the lowest level peer group consisting of a collection of switches. The peer groups are organized hierarchically into higher levels of peer groups which are parents of the lower layer peer groups. Each peer group has a peer group leader that performs a set of special functions for the group.

The signaling protocol uses information gathered by PNNI routing to do the designated transit list (DTL) processing and crankback. The crankback mechanism enables a connection that is blocked along a selected path to be rolled back to the node earlier in the path where the DTL was created; this node will choose another path to the desired destination (i.e, it will create another DTL).

The ATM LAN
Emulation Service

9.1 Introduction

One of the primary areas ATM is used is to interconnect legacy enter-prise networks, as discussed in Chapter 1. However, most legacy net-works operate in a connectionless access mode while the ATM network operates in a connection-oriented mode. The ATM Forum has issued the LAN Emulation (or LANE) specification that defines mechanisms that permit legacy networks to coexist with the ATM network, thereby protecting the huge investments made in legacy networks.

LAN emulation allows the ATM network to emulate the connec-tionless nature of a LAN [54]. It seamlessly allows end stations in one legacy LAN to access applications and other end stations in another legacy LAN. An emulated LAN (ELAN) permits the transfer of user frames between all the ELAN users in a connectionless manner, as in a physical LAN, via the ATM network. All the users on one ELAN use the same MAC layer protocol; an emulated LAN is either an Ethernet/IEEE 802.3 LAN or an IEEE 802.5 (token ring) LAN. Several emulated LANs can be configured within the same ATM network and an end sta-tion can belong to multiple emulated LANs. However, traffic originat-ing from one emulated LAN cannot cross the boundaries of that LAN. Such traffic has to pass through a router in order to get into the other ELAN. LANE supports both point-to-point (or unicast) connections and point-to-multipoint (multicast and broadcast) connections.

9.2 LANE Protocol Stack

The function of LAN emulation is to hide the complexity of call setup from the user and provide emulated services similar to the broadcast

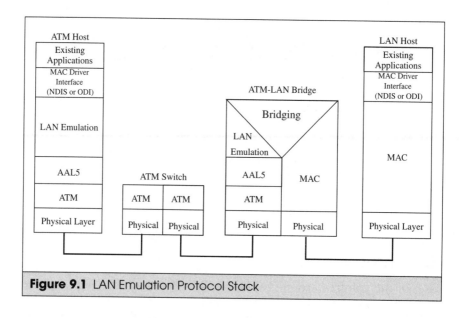

Figure 9.1 LAN Emulation Protocol Stack

operation of the conventional LAN. Figure 9.1 shows the protocol stack for LAN emulation. As this figure illustrates, the LAN emulation layer is the layer above the ATM adaptation layer type 5 in the ATM host since LAN traffic is an AAL5 type. In the ATM-to-LAN bridge, the LAN emulation layer is also the layer above the ATM adaptation layer.

One of the goals in defining the LAN emulation service is to ensure that it requires no modification to higher layer protocols. The LAN emulation service communicates with application software through exisiting MAC drivers such as NDIS driver or ODI driver, thereby fooling the application software into believing that it is talking to a standard network adapter driver. (NDIS, which stands for Network Driver Interface Specification, was developed by Microsoft for writing hardware-independent drivers. Similarly, ODI (Open Datalink Interface) is the Novell standard for hardware-independent drivers.)

9.3 LANE Components

LAN emulation operates in a client-server mode. An emulated LAN consists of multiple **LAN emulation clients** (LECs) and one LAN emulation service. The LECs interact with the LAN emulation service across the UNI. This interface is popularly referred to as **LAN emulation UNI** (LUNI). A LAN emulation client is the entity in a legacy LAN that performs data forwarding and address resolution. It is also an end station in the ATM network which may be a bridge or router representing a set of users on a legacy LAN that are identified by their MAC addresses. A LEC may also be a workstation that is directly attached to the ATM network.

The components of the LAN emulation service are as follows:

1. The **LAN emulation server** (LES) provides a facility for registering and resolving MAC addresses; it also responds to LEC queries. Each emulated LAN has one LES.
2. The **broadcast and unknown server** (BUS) handles all multicast transmissions and unicasts the initial packets that are sent by a LEC before a connection to the target ATM address has been established. Each emulated LAN has one BUS.
3. The **LAN emulation configuration server** (LECS) assigns the LECs to the different emulated LANs. It does this by providing each LEC with the ATM address of the LES for the emulated LAN assigned to it. One LECS serves one network that consists of many emulated LANs.

The LES and BUS functionalities for an emulated LAN can be implemented in the same device. Figure 9.2 illustrates the relationships between the different LANE components. This figure represents the view of LANE from a single emulated LAN perspective.

Figure 9.3 shows a more global view of LANE where the LECS resides outside each emulated LAN. The arrows show how the different LANE components interact through connections that are set up between them. This is explained later in this chapter.

9.4 Principles of LAN Emulation

The ATM Forum LAN Emulation Version 1.0 operates in the following manner: First, there is a **configuration phase,** during which the LECs

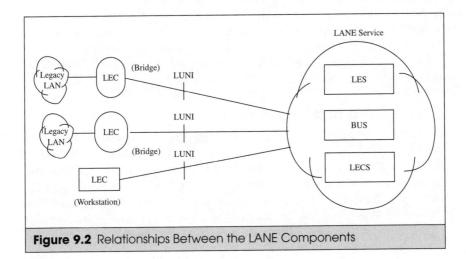

Figure 9.2 Relationships Between the LANE Components

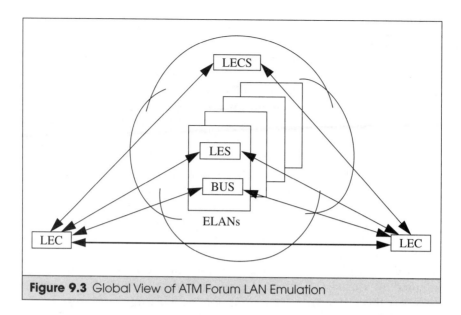

Figure 9.3 Global View of ATM Forum LAN Emulation

determine the ATM address of their LES. Second, there is a **joining and registration phase,** when a LEC joins an emulated LAN and, optionally, registers the MAC addresses of the end stations it represents with the LES for that emulated LAN. Finally, there is an **address resolution phase,** when a LEC (that has a packet with only the MAC address of the destination end station and not its ATM network address) attempts to map this MAC address into an ATM network address.

9.4.1 Configuration

During the configuration phase, a LEC establishes a bidirectional point-to-point connection to the LECS called the **Configuration Direct Virtual Channel Connection**. Using this virtual channel connection (VCC), the LEC requests the ATM address of the LES for the emulated LAN it wants to join. The LECS returns the ATM address of the LES on the same VCC.

9.4.2 Joining and Registration

During the joining and registration phase, the LEC establishes a bidirectional point-to-point connection to the LES called the **Control Direct VCC** and requests to join the ELAN served by the LES. If the procedure is successfully completed, the LEC is assigned a unique LEC identifier (LEC ID). The LES may optionally establish a **Control Distribute VCC** as a point-to-multipoint or a unidirectional point-to-point connection to the LEC. The LES will also provide the LEC with the

ATM address of the BUS that serves the ELAN when requested by the LEC. The LEC then establishes a bidirectional point-to-point connection to the BUS called the **Multicast Send VCC.** This virtual channel connection is used to send multicast data and the initial unicast packet, as will be explained later. The BUS sets up a connection to the LEC called the **Multicast Forward VCC,** which may be used for distributing data from the BUS. This can be either a point-to-multipoint VCC or a unidirectional point-to-point VCC. After joining the LAN, the LEC may register any number of MAC addresses with the LES, one at a time. It may also elect to do proxy registration in which no individual MAC addresses are registered with the LES. The proxy registration is done at the same time the LEC joins the emulated LAN; the registration cannot be changed from proxy to explicit registration once it is done.

9.4.3 Address Resolution

End stations are usually known by their MAC addresses. However, only ATM addresses can be used for connection setup in the ATM network. Address resolution is the process of mapping these MAC addresses into ATM addresses. When a LEC receives a packet whose destination LEC is unknown, it sends a **LAN emulation address resolution protocol** (LE_ARP) request to the LES over its Control Direct VCC. The LE_ARP request essentially tells the LES to provide the LEC issuing the request (RQ) with the ATM address of the LEC that "owns" the destination end station with the included MAC address. If that MAC address has been registered with the LES, the latter will issue an LE_ARP reply, indicating the ATM address of the LEC for the target end station. If the MAC address has not been registered with the LES, it will forward the LE_ARP request to all the LECs that did proxy registration. When the appropriate LEC responds to the LE_ARP request, the LES forwards the LE_ARP reply (RP) to the LEC that issued the initial LE_ARP request. The LEC will then initiate the setup of a bidirectional point-to-point connection called the **Data Direct VCC** between itself and the target LEC.

Figure 9.4 is a summary of the steps involved in LANE configuration, registration, and data forwarding between two LECs, LEC A and LEC B, both of which belong to the same ELAN.

9.5 Example of LANE Operation

When a LEC receives a packet destined for an end station whose ATM address is not known, it attempts to resolve the destination address with the LES for its emulated LAN by sending an LE_ARP request to the LES over its Control Direct VCC, as discussed earlier. If that MAC address has been registered with the LES, the LES will issue an LE_ARP

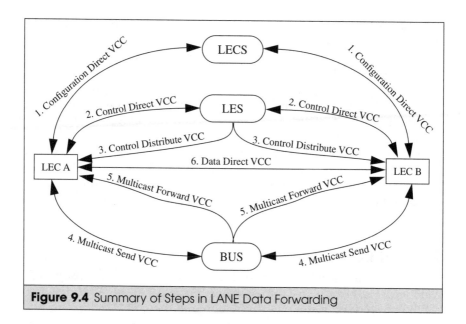

Figure 9.4 Summary of Steps in LANE Data Forwarding

reply indicating the ATM address of the LEC for the target end station. If the MAC address has not been registered with the LES, it will forward the LE_ARP request to all the LECs that perform proxy registration. When the appropriate LEC responds to the LE_ARP request, the LES forwards the LE_ARP reply (RP) to the LEC that issued the initial LE_ARP request. The LEC will then initiate the setup of a bidirectional point-to-point Data Direct VCC between itself and the target LEC. After initiating the setup request, the LEC may forward the packet to the BUS for unicasting to the destination LEC whose address has been appended on the packet. (This is an optional feature in the ATM Forum specification.)

The ATM Forum specification states that the packet can also be sent to the BUS prior to sending the SETUP message. If the initial packet was forwarded to the BUS, then after the Data Direct VCC has been set up, the LEC may issue a FLUSH message via the BUS before any data can be sent on the Data Direct VCC. An alternative to sending the FLUSH message is to wait for a length of time that the ATM Forum specification calls "path switching delay" before data can be sent to Data Direct VCC.

The purpose of the FLUSH message (or waiting for the path switching delay) is to ensure that packets sent by the source end station are received by the destination end station in the correct order when the source end station switches from the Multicast Send VCC (destined for the BUS) to the Data Direct VCC. The destination LEC is required to send a reply to a FLUSH message through the LES. If there is no

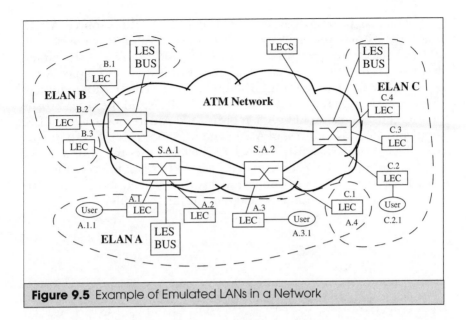

Figure 9.5 Example of Emulated LANs in a Network

LE_ARP response from the LES, the LEC forwards the packet to the BUS. The BUS will forward the packet to all the LECs.

Consider the network shown in Figure 9.5 in which there are three emulated LANs called ELAN A, ELAN B, and ELAN C. LEC A.4 is in both ELAN A and ELAN C and, therefore, has the additional address C.1. A packet generated by an end station A.1.1 on ELAN A is destined for an end station A.3.1 on the same ELAN but is attached to a different LEC. The source end station sends the packet to the source LEC (LEC A.1), which then attempts to resolve the MAC address of the destination end station with the LES for the ELAN A. The LES returns the ATM address of LEC A.3 to LEC A.1 since A.3.1 is attached to A.3. LEC A.1 then initiates a call setup request to the network through the ATM switch S.A.1. Switch S.A.1 passes the message to switch S.A.2. Switch S.A.2 passes the message to LEC A.3, which returns a CONNECT message to LEC A.1 via S.A.2 and S.A.1. After LEC A.1 has received the CONNECT message, it will forward the READY_INDICATE message to LEC A.3.1 along the same path that the SETUP and CONNECT messages took. The connection is established between the two LECs.

After sending the SETUP request, LEC A.1 drops the packet on the Multicast Send VCC for the BUS to unicast to the LEC A.3 whose address has now been appended on the packet. After the connection has been established, LEC A.1 sends a FLUSH message to the BUS, which forwards it to LEC A.3. The latter returns a FLUSH response to LEC A.1, and all transactions through the BUS are terminated between LEC A.1 and LEC A.3 relative to that source MAC address-destination MAC address pair.

Note that prior to packet arrival at LEC A.1, the source A.1.1, which knows only the network layer address of A.3.1 (such as the IP address), has to resolve this address to the MAC address of the target destination. In the case of an IP address, this is done as follows: A.1.1 issues an IP ARP request for A.3.1's MAC address. The IP ARP request is received by LEC A.1, which forwards it to the BUS and the latter broadcasts it. The destination LEC, A.3, returns an IP ARP response to the BUS, supplying the MAC address of A.3.1. The BUS forwards the response to A.1, which in turn forwards it to A.1.1. The latter uses the MAC address to send the intended packet to A.3.1 via LEC A.1. On receiving the packet, A.1 initiates the LAN emulation service described above. Figure 9.6 illustrates the information flow diagram for this example.

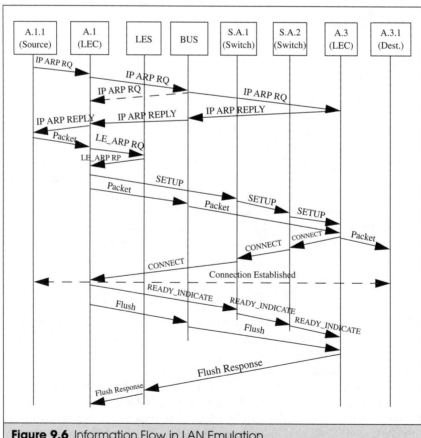

Figure 9.6 Information Flow in LAN Emulation

9.6 Summary

The ATM LAN emulation service enables legacy systems to use an ATM network in a transparent manner. It essentially hides the ATM network from these systems, thereby requiring no modification to their protocol stacks. Unfortunately, this causes the QoS features of the ATM to be hidden from these systems. As a result of this, LAN emulation cannot be used for LAN-based, delay-sensitive applications that may require some QoS guarantee.

The emulated LAN is functionally a single LAN segment; this means that an emulated LAN is either an Ethernet or a token ring network. Therefore, traffic that has to cross emulated LAN boundaries must go through a router.

10

IP Over ATM

10.1 Introduction

The Internet suite of protocols has become the *de facto* standard for open systems. Consequently, many legacy systems use the IP as their network layer protocol. IP over ATM is a service that provides a mechanism by which IP can be transported over the ATM network. It specifies two processes: **packet encapsulation** and **address resolution**.

10.2 Packet Encapsulation

Packet encapsulation is a mechanism that permits multiple packet types to be multiplexed on the same connection at the network layer. The advantage of packet encapsulation is that it permits connection reuse and as a result, reduces connection setup time. It works by appending a multiplexing field that enables the receiving node to identify the packet type. The encapsulated packet is carried over ATM AAL5. Two methods of packet encapsulation are discussed in RFC 1483 [55]:

- LLC/SNAP encapsulation
- VC multiplexing

LLC/SNAP encapsulation is used when several protocols are carried over the same VC. In this scheme, the protocol is identified by prefixing the IP packet with an IEEE 802.2 logical link control (LLC) header, followed by an IEEE 802.1a Subnetwork Attachment Point (SNAP) header. The SNAP consists of two subfields: a 3-octet Organizationally Unique Identifer (OUI) that administers the meaning of the following

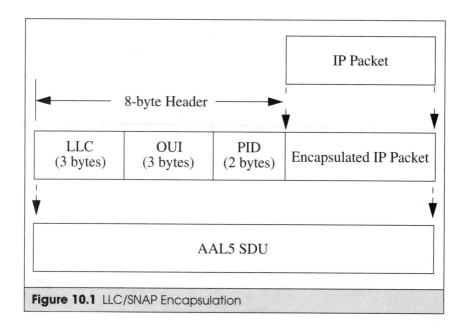

Figure 10.1 LLC/SNAP Encapsulation

2-octet Protocol Identifier (PID). For example, the OUI value 0x00-00-00 specifies that the PID is an EtherType. An LLC/SNAP encapsulated IP packet appears as in Figure 10.1, which shows an AAL5 SDU [56].

The maximum transfer unit (MTU) size is standardized at 9180 bytes, excluding the 8-byte LLC/SNAP header. However, the MTU size can be negotiated up to 64 kbytes. LLC/SNAP encapsulation is the default scheme for IP over ATM.

In VC multiplexing, each protocol is carried over a separate VC with the protocol type specified at connection setup. Thus, VC multiplexing results in minimal bandwidth and processing overhead.

There are variations of packet encapsulation and many of them are still under development. The goal of this chapter is to discuss the classical model and summarize the other models that are essentially extensions to the classical model.

10.3 Address Resolution

The "classical" view of an IP network is one in which clusters of IP nodes (end systems and routers) with similar subnet addresses are connected to nodes outside their cluster by IP routers. The IETF maintained this view in its "Classical IP over ATM" model defined in RFC 1577 [57]. The model groups IP nodes in an ATM network into logical IP subnets (LIS). The nodes in one LIS communicate with those outside their LIS through an IP router. Within each LIS is a component called the **ATM address resolution protocol server** (ATMARP server) that performs directory services function for the nodes in the LIS. Each node is configured with the ATM address of its ATMARP server. The address resolution process works in a client/server manner, with the nodes as the clients.

When a node comes up, it uses the configured address to establish a connection to the ATMARP server for its LIS. On detecting the connection from the new client, the server sends an Inverse ARP [58] request to the client requesting the client's IP address since it knows the client's ATM address through the connection. When it receives a response from the client, the ATMARP server stores the client's IP and ATM addresses in its ATMARP table.

Before a client in a LIS can communicate with another client in the same LIS, it must resolve the latter's IP address to its ATM address. To do this, it sends an ATMARP request to the ATMARP server which responds with the target client's ATM address, if it is found in the ATMARP table. Otherwise, it returns an ATM_NAK response which indicates that the target client is not registered. Once the client has received the target client's ATM address, it can set up a connection to the latter. The ATMARP table entries are valid for 20 minutes, after which an entry is deleted. It is the responsibility of a client to refresh its entry by using the procedure described earlier to register with the ATMARP server.

An example of the Classical IP over ATM network architecture is in Figure 10.2.

In this figure, two routers are configured as members of two LISs, and the clients on different subnets must communicate via such routers. For example, a client in LIS 1 that wants to communicate with a client in LIS 2 must go through Router 1 even though a direct VC can be established between the two clients over the ATM network.

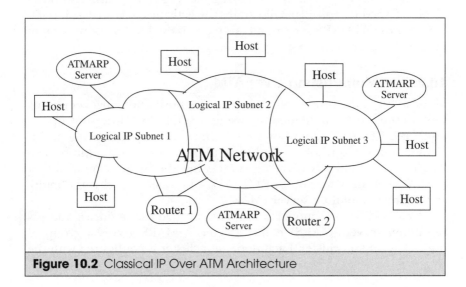

Figure 10.2 Classical IP Over ATM Architecture

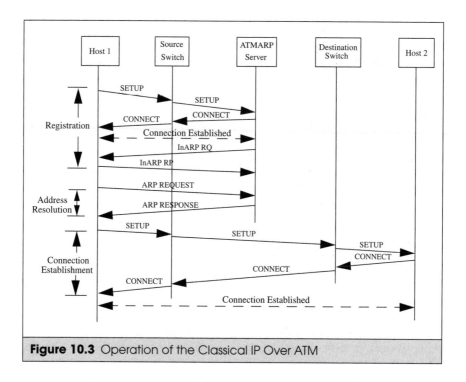

Figure 10.3 Operation of the Classical IP Over ATM

Figure 10.3 is an information flow diagram that summarizes the address resolution process of the Classical IP over ATM.

In this figure, Host 1 first establishes a connection to its LIS ATMARP server and then resolves an address for Host 2 in the same LIS. This diagram assumes that the two clients are attached to different switches within the LIS and that Host 2 had registered earlier with the ATMARP server. Figure 10.3 illustrates the activities of Host 1 as it registers with the ATMARP server and attempts to establish a connection to Host 2.

10.3.1 IP Multicasting Over ATM

Multicasting is the process whereby a source host sends a packet to multiple destinations simultaneously using a single local transmit operation [59]. RFC 1577 does not address the issue of multicasting and it cannot be used to resolve a multicast address to an ATM address. The Internet community is currently addressing the issue of multicasting over ATM as an extension to RFC 1577. The basic model is the **multicast address resolution server** (MARS) model [59].

In a MARS-based model, a new entity called the **multicast address resolution server** (MARS) is introduced. A MARS serves a group of nodes known as a **cluster**. Each node in a cluster is configured with the

ATM address of the MARS. A MARS can support only one cluster, and a MARS does not take part in the actual multicasting of the layer 3 data packets. Each LIS should be served by a separate MARS, thereby ensuring one-to-one mapping between cluster and unicast LIS [59]. Traffic belonging to hosts in different clusters passes through an inter-cluster device which is usually a router that has logical interfaces to both clusters.

When a host wants to join a cluster, it establishes a bidirectional point-to-point virtual channel (VC) to the MARS for the cluster. The VC is used to send queries to, and receive replies from, the MARS. The VC has an associated timer and is dismantled if not used within a configurable period of time. When the host joins the cluster, the MARS adds the host to a point-to-multipoint VC, called the **ClusterControlVC**. With the ClusterControlVC configured this way, the cluster takes the form of a tree in which all registered clients are leaves and the MARS is the root. The MARS distributes cluster membership update information to the cluster members over this VC. Figure 10.4 shows the logical configuration of an ATM network with two clusters.

When a host wants to transmit to its multicast group, it issues a MARS_REQUEST message to the MARS. If no other host has registered with the MARS, the MARS returns a MARS_NACK to the host and the IP packet is silently discarded. If at least one other host has registered with the MARS, the MARS returns a MARS-MULTI message that contains the set of ATM addresses of the other hosts that have registered with the MARS. Using this address set, the requesting host establishes a point-to-multipoint connection to the set of addresses.

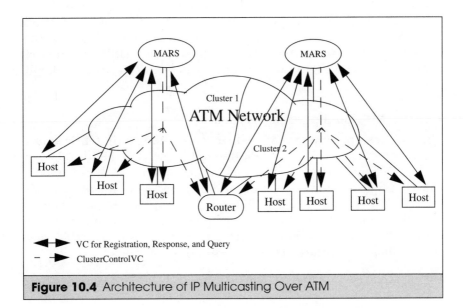

Figure 10.4 Architecture of IP Multicasting Over ATM

In another model, a host may establish a connection to an intermediate node called the **multicast server** (MCS) which is responsible for establishing and managing a point-to-multipoint VC to the desired destinations. In this case, what the MARS returns to the requesting host is the ATM address of the MCS that serves the group. The host then sets up a point-to-point connection to the MCS and transmits its multicast packet to the MCS which, as a proxy agent, uses a point-to-multipoint VC to forward the data to the group members. The model permits more than one MCS in a LIS.

10.3.2 Next Hop Resolution Protocol

As discussed above, if a client in one LIS wants to communicate with another client in another LIS, it must go through a router that is a member of multiple logical IP subnets. This is a limitation of the model because the router becomes a bottleneck. The **Next Hop Resolution Protocol** (NHRP) [60] is designed to address this limitation; it attempts to prevent the extra hops involved in the routing of IP packets.

NHRP is designed for non-broadcast multi-access (NBMA) networks, which are essentially those networks that allow multiple hosts to be attached to it but does not permit the use of broadcasting, as in local area networks. Examples of NBMA networks are X.25 and ATM networks. The primary component of the NHRP is the NHRP server (NHS). An NHS serves a set of hosts (or NHRP stations) attached to the NBMA network and answers NHRP resolution requests from these stations.

The network is partitioned into administrative domains called **logical NBMA subnets** (LNS), and each LNS is served by an NHS which performs IP address to ATM address mapping for the stations in its LNS. Each station is configured with the ATM address of its domain's NHS. When a station comes up, it establishes a point-to-point VC to the NHS and registers with the NHS by sending an NHRP Registration Request. The NHS responds by returning an NHRP Registration Reply to the station.

10.3.2.1 NHS Configuration Modes

The NHSs can be configured in either **server mode** or in **fabric mode.** In server mode, each NHS is statically configured with the IP addresses of all the clients served by every NHS in the network. In fabric mode, an NHS acquires knowledge of the addresses served by the other NHSs through intra-LNS and inter-LNS routing protocols. The server mode is good for small networks while the fabric mode is good for medium to large networks. The NHRP servers maintain a routing table that enables them to forward NHRP address resolution requests.

10.3.2.2 NHRP Address Resolution

When a station has an IP packet to transmit, it sends an NHRP Resolution Request IP packet to the NHS for its LNS, requesting the ATM address of the desired destination. If the destination is served by the NHS, it returns the ATM address in an NHRP Resolution Reply packet, and the requesting station can then establish a direct connection to the destination. If the destination is not served by the NHS, or the destination address is not in the NHRP server's cache, the NHS uses a well-defined routing algorithm to forward the request to another NHS. Any NHS that receives such a request will determine if it knows the address of the destination. If it does not, it forwards it to another NHS until the request reaches the NHS that serves the destination. If an NHS knows the destination's ATM address, it returns the address in an NHRP Resolution Reply packet that is required to traverse the reverse route taken by the request packet. Each NHS that receives a reply packet can cache the address for future use.

There are two types of replies that may be requested: **authoritative** and **non-authoritative**. An authoritative reply is one that is generated by the NHS serving the desired destination. In this case, no transit NHS may use its cached information to reply to the request. A non-authoritative reply is one generated by a transit NHS that has resolved the destination's address with the information in its cache.

Sometimes an NHRP Resolution Reply may not have to traverse the NHSs that forwarded the NHRP Resolution Request. It may be returned directly to the source that initiated the request. The purpose of this direct reply is to reduce the response time of the NHRP Resolution Request. This scheme is typically the case when

- the NHS has an existing VCC to the initiator.
- the NHRP Resolution Request initiator has not included the **NHRP Reverse Transit NHS record extension,** which is a list of NHSs through which a reply has to traverse.
- the authoritative policy permits a direct communication between the NHS and the NHRP Resolution Request initiator.

Figure 10.5 illustrates the operation of the NHRP. There are four logical NBMA subnets in the network, each of which is served by an NHS. This figure illustrates the two cases where authoritative and non-authoritative NHRP requests are required. The figure assumes that NHS 1 wants to resolve an address of a destination served by NHS 4 and that NHS 2, which lies on the route from NHS 1 to NHS 4, has cached this address by some means.

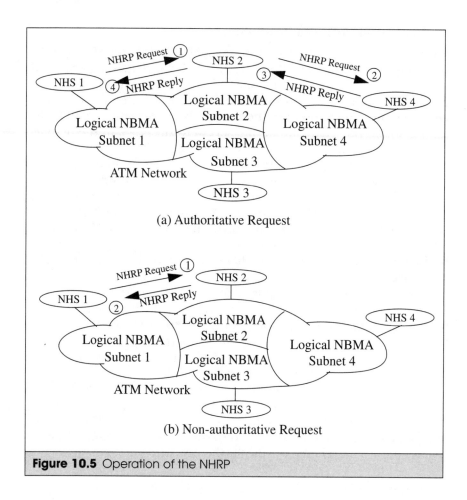

Figure 10.5 Operation of the NHRP

10.4 Internet Integrated Services

The Internet was designed to handle the "best effort" delivery of IP traffic; it was not designed to handle such real-time traffic as voice and video that demand guaranteed quality of service. With many workstations equipped to handle multimedia service and the availability of digital and audio applications, the need to introduce real-time traffic with guaranteed QoS has become real. The Internet Engineering Task Force (IETF) is currently developing new protocols that will enable the Internet to provide the guaranteed QoS to real-time traffic while maintaining the best effort service for the non-real-time traffic. Integrated services (IS) is a new service model for the Internet that includes best-effort services, real-time services, and controlled link sharing [61]. The IS model essentially represents the changes to classical IP that will enable it to support multimedia services.

Two capabilities are required for the Internet to support IS [62]:

1. Individual network elements (subnets and IP routers) along the path taken by an application's data packets must support mechanisms to control the QoS delivered to the packets.
2. A mechanism must be provided for an application's requirements to be communicated to the network elements along the path taken by the application's packets, in a manner similar to the signaling used in switched networks.

In the IS model, the first requirement is provided by the QoS control services, and the second requirement is provided by the **Resource Reservation Protocol** (RSVP) [63]. The work on the QoS control services is still in progress; four service classes have been proposed:

- **Guaranteed delay service** [64]: provides firm bounds on the maximum end-to-end packet transfer delay for each session using the service.
- **Controlled delay service** [65]: offers applications several levels of delay to choose from.
- **Predictive service** [66]: offers applications low packet loss service and a maximum bound on end-to-end delay.
- **Controlled-load service** [67]: offers a level of service that closely approximates the QoS that the same flow would receive from an unloaded network; it uses admission control to ensure that this service is received even when the network is overloaded.

10.4.1 RSVP

The RSVP [63] is a receiver-initiated control protocol that enables network resources to be reserved for a connectionless data stream in the Internet. "Receiver-initiated" refers to the host where a resource is located, and which ultimately receives requests for resource allocation, that initiates communication with interested parties by advertising the services it can provide. It solicits reservations for resources from interested parties (or nodes). This is different from ATM UNI signaling protocols that are sender-initiated; the party that wishes to send some data initiates the communication process by requesting resources from the network. Some of the features of RSVP are as follows:

1. RSVP has a "soft state" feature that allows information to time out rather than be explicitly deleted. Periodic refresh messages are generated to maintain the state. The state automatically times out and is deleted if no refresh messages are received.
2. RSVP permits heterogeneous reservations within a multicast.

3. RSVP permits QoS changes to be made dynamically.

4. RSVP permits multiple reservation styles to fit a variety of applications.

10.4.1.1 Operation of the RSVP

There are two basic types of messages in the RSVP: PATH and RESV. PATH messages are sent "downstream" by a sender to convey information to the receivers before any reservation can be made. A PATH message carries information about the source traffic parameters such as mean bit rate. No resources are reserved until the receivers, using the information contained in the PATH message, send RESV messages "upstream" (usually along the reverse path of the PATH message) to make reservation for specific resources.

Multiple receivers can send RESV messages toward the same source(s), and the quantities of the resources requested by these receivers may be different. A node that receives such requests merges them and generates one RESV message which it forwards toward the source(s). This new RESV message carries the maximum of the resource quantities contained in the incoming reservation requests.

An RSVP reservation request consists of a **flow descriptor** that is made up of a **flowspec** and a **filter spec**. The flowspec specifies a desired QoS while the filter spec is used to configure the packet classifier based on the reservation style. Any node that is capable of resource reservation passes incoming data packets through a **packet classifier,** which determines the route and the QoS class of each packet. For each outgoing interface, a **packet scheduler** then makes forwarding decisions for each packet to achieve the promised QoS. When an intermediate node receives an RSVP reservation request message, it takes two actions:

1. **Make a reservation:** The flowspec and filter spec are used by the admission control and policy control systems to determine whether to admit or reject the request. If the request is rejected, an error message is returned to the requester. If admitted, the node uses the flowspec to set up the packet scheduler for the desired QoS and the flow filter to set the packet classifier to select the appropriate data packets.

2. **Forward the request upstream:** The request message is forwarded upstream toward the appropriate sender(s).

In RSVP a **flow** is the set of data packets that receive the QoS defined by the flowspec and a **session** is a data flow with a particular destination and transport layer protocol.

The basic RSVP reservation model is **one pass**. Here, a receiver sends an RESV message upstream and each node in the path either accepts or rejects the request. The receiver has no way of determining the resulting end-to-end service. An enhanced service model is the **one**

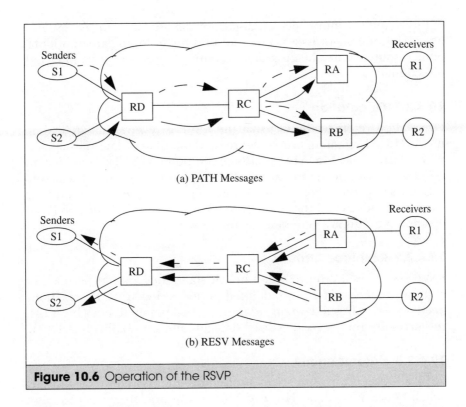

(a) PATH Messages

(b) RESV Messages

Figure 10.6 Operation of the RSVP

pass with advertising (OPWA) in which control packets are sent downstream, following the data paths, to gather information that may be used to predict end-to-end QoS. The results, called **advertisements,** are delivered by RSVP to the receiver hosts and may be used by them to construct or dynamically adjust an appropriate reservation request.

Figure 10.6 illustrates the operation of the RSVP. There are four routers: RA, RB, RC, and RD. There are two senders: S1 and S2, and there are two receivers: R1 and R2. This figure illustrates how intermediate router RC forwards only one RESV message for each sender, even though it received two. This illustrates the **merge** operation. Figure 10.6 assumes that all routers on the path of the RESV messages have admitted the calls.

10.4.2 IS Over ATM

There are several differences between the operation of the IS Internet and the ATM network. Before IS over ATM can be possible, these differences need to be resolved. Most of the issues arise from the fact that RSVP, the signaling protocol for IS, is based on a paradigm that is different from that of the ATM UNI signaling. These issues are currently being addressed by the IETF and are summarized here for completeness of this chapter. A more detailed discussion can be found in [68, 69, 70]. Essentially, the major issues center around the following areas: orientation, resource state, heterogeneity, routing, QoS renegotiation, and directionality.

10.4.2.1 Orientation

Orientation refers to the fact that the RSVP is receiver-initiated while the ATM UNI signaling protocols are sender-initiated. This mismatch is particularly critical in ATM point-to-multipoint VCs. The end system requesting a connection in an ATM network reserves resources at connection setup time. For point-to-multipoint calls, the sender initiates connection setup and the resource reservation. In RSVP, the RSVP reservation requests are generated by the receiver.

10.4.2.2 Resource State

RSVP resources are represented in soft state; they are not permanent and they time out after a predefined period of inactivity. Reservations need to be refreshed to prevent their being timed out. In ATM, resources are represented by hard state and must be explicitly deleted.

10.4.2.3 Heterogeneity

RSVP allows a receiver to select a subset of senders and to dynamically switch between senders. This capability is not available in ATM. Also, multiple receivers may request different Rspecs within a single session in RSVP but the amount of requested resources may differ from one hop to the next. In ATM, the same QoS allocation must be made for all leaves in a point-to-multipoint VC.

10.4.2.4 Routing

In ATM, the route setup and resource reservation are done at the same time when the connection is being established. In RSVP, route setup and resource reservation are done at different times.

10.4.2.5 QoS Renegotiation

Because of its soft state approach to resource reservation, RSVP allows changes to be made at any time in the QoS parameters of a flow. In ATM, the QoS is fixed for the duration of a connection.

10.4.2.6 Directionality

In RSVP, resources are reserved in one direction only. In ATM, connections are bidirectional in point-to-point calls and unidirectional in point-to-multipoint calls. In ATM, resources are reserved in both directions for point-to-point calls and in only one direction for point-to-multipoint calls.

10.5 Summary

This chapter presented the main features of the IP over ATM protocols, including the Next Hop Resolution Protocol (NHRP). This is an active and developing area within the IETF. Consequently most of the issues have yet to be resolved. In particular, the IETF integrated services over ATM is somewhat in its infancy. The Resource Reservation Protocol (RSVP) is the signaling protocol for the IETF integrated services. This chapter has highlighted the major issues that are being addressed for RSVP over ATM.

CHAPTER 11

Multiprotocol Over ATM

11.1 Introduction

The ATM LAN emulation hides the layers above layer 2 from the ATM fabric. Consequently, applications running over a LAN emulation network cannot take advantage of the quality of service (QoS) capabilities of the ATM. Also, in ATM LAN emulation, the address resolution protocol overhead is high. Typically, an IP address to MAC-layer address mapping is first done, then a MAC-layer address to ATM address resolution is performed. While the **IP over ATM** reduces this overhead by the use of the ATM address resolution protocol (ATMARP) server, it deals with only the IP.

The **multiprotocol over ATM** (MPOA) [71] is a service that is designed to provide a unified model for overlaying layer 3 protocols on ATM. It permits direct ATM connections (or shortcuts) between MPOA devices. By permitting the direct connection between MPOA devices, it takes full advantage of the ATM quality of service features. MPOA integrates the IETF Next Hop Resolution Protocol (NHRP) and the ATM Forum LAN emulation into its address resolution scheme and has, in some cases, made extensions to these protocols to adapt them to the specific requirements of the multiprotocol over ATM. MPOA can be viewed as a client/server system in which a group of network-based servers provides service to edge-attached clients.

11.2 MPOA Components

The major components of MPOA are:

- **Edge device** (ED): A physical device that is capable of forwarding packets between legacy systems and the ATM network at a layer 3 protocol.

139

- **ATM-attached host** (AH): An MPOA capable device that is directly connected to the ATM network.

- **Internetwork address subgroup** (IASG): A range of internetwork layer addresses summarized into an internetwork layer routing protocol. It is uniquely identified by the combination of the internetwork layer protocol used, the internetwork address prefix, and the internetwork address prefix range. An IASG is identified by an IASG identifier (IASGid).

- **Route server** (RS): A physical entity that runs layer 3 routing protocols and communicates with other MPOA devices to resolve layer 3 addresses to ATM addresses. It can also forward traffic from one IASG to another, from an MPOA client in one IASG to another IASG, and from one MPOA client in one IASG to an MPOA client in another IASG. It acts as the NHRP next hop server (NHS) in inter-IASG address resolution.

- **MPOA configuration server:** An entity that provides configuration information to both MPOA clients and MPOA servers. It can be the same as the LAN emulation configuration server.

- **MPOA client** (MPC): A protocol entity that implements the client side of the MPOA protocol. An MPC is an edge device or ATM-attached host.

- **MPOA server** (MPS): A protocol entity that implements the server side of the MPOA protocol. MPS includes the RS and the MPOA configuration server. (In earlier versions of the MPOA baseline document, many types of servers were defined. However, the latest versions tend to concentrate most of the server functionalities on the RS.)

Figure 11.1 shows the MPOA architecture with a sample configuration. In this configuration there are three internetwork address subgroups, labelled IASG1, IASG2, and IASG3; one MPOA configuration server; two route servers, labelled RS1 and RS2, in which RS1 is a member of IASG1 and IASG2 and RS2 is a member of IASG2 and IASG3; ATM-attached hosts, labelled AH1.1, AH1.2, etc.; and edge devices, labelled ED1.1, ED1.2, etc. The edge devices connect legacy networks to the ATM network. As described in the next section, the default data transfer scheme in MPOA is the ATM LAN emulation and each IASG has a LES/BUS pair associated with it. In Figure 11.1 a LES/BUS pair is shown for each IASG.

11.3 Operation of the MPOA

An MPOA server's **service area** consists of an MPOA server and the set of MPOA clients served by that server. An IASG is essentially an MPOA

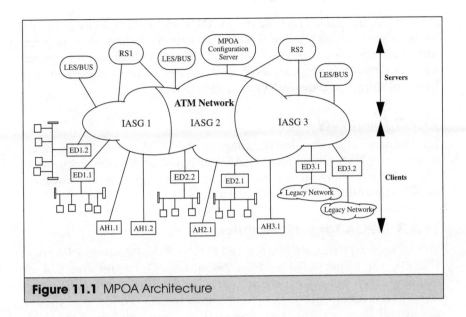

Figure 11.1 MPOA Architecture

server's service area. Each IASG is associated with exactly one emulated LAN. The MPOA system provides four basic services:

1. **Configuration:** A process that ensures all functional groups have the appropriate set of information to run MPOA.
2. **Discovery:** A process that enables LANE-attached MPOA components to learn of each other's existence and functional type.
3. **MPOA target resolution:** The process of determining the route description, given a destination network layer address.
4. **Data delivery:** The process of getting the data from one MPOA client to another.

The configuration server is expected to be the same entity that provides configuration service for LAN emulation service. Each MPOA entity (MPS or MPC) is configured with the ATM address of its configuration server. Every edge device and route server is required to be a member of an emulated LAN (ELAN).

11.3.1 Configuration

When an MPOA server comes up, it obtains from the configuration server its IASG, the protocol of the IASG, the IASGid, the address prefix of the IASG, and the name of emulated LAN (ELAN) that is participating in its IASG. Similarly, when an MPOA client comes up, it obtains from the configuration server the protocol for the ELAN the client is bridging to, the packet rate for the ELAN, and the ATM addresses of the route servers to which it can forward packets. The client then registers with the route servers by establishing an **RSend virtual channel connection (VCC)** to each route server. A route server confirms the registration by establishing an **RForward VCC** to the client.

11.3.2 Discovery

LAN emulation service devices attached to MPOA networks use extensions of the LAN emulation LE_ARP protocol to discover each other. The information obtained from the discovery process includes the device type and the ATM address of a device.

11.3.3 MPOA Target Resolution

MPOA uses an extension of the IETF Next Hop Resolution Protocol (NHRP) for target ATM address resolution. The extension can be explained as follows: In the traditional NHRP, when an NHRP server (NHS) receives an ARP request and knows the ATM address of the target, it will issue an ARP response that contains the requested ATM address. MPOA operates slightly differently from the traditional method in cases involving an edge device. In MPOA, when the route server that serves the target IASG receives an ARP request, the route server is required to send the request to the edge device rather than furnish the ATM address of the edge device. The edge device responds to the ARP request and in this way is alerted to an impending packet arrival. In the case where the final edge device is behind another edge device, the **cache imposition protocol** [71] is used to extend the query to the desired final destination. The cache imposition protocol ensures that the source ATM address is preserved in NHRP query requests.

11.3.4 Data Transfer

All frames transmitted over ATM by MPOA devices use the RFC 1483 LLC/SNAP header [55]. There are two ways in which unicast data can be handled in an MPOA system:

- default flow
- shortcut flow

The default data transfer uses the ATM LAN emulation based on the MAC address of the packet. This mode is used when shortcuts do not exist. If the destination end system is outside the source MPC's ELAN, the MPC forwards the packet via the RSend VCC to a route server. The route server has the responsibility to send the packet to its destination via the RForward VCC, if the route server serves the IASG of the target.

However, if the route server does not serve the IASG in which the target is located, it forwards the packet via LAN emulation to another route server that will continue this LAN emulation forwarding process until the packet reaches the target.

Packets enter the MPOA at the MPCs at the edge of the network (i.e., ingress MPCs). An MPC examines its cache to see if it has the address pair (MAC address, Layer 3 address). If the pair is found and a VCC exists, the packet is stripped of its MAC header. Then it is encapsulated using the appropriate layer 3 protocol encapsulation and sent over the shortcut VCC. If the address pair is found in the cache but no VCC exists, the packet is sent via LANE. In this case, the MPC is required to keep a tally of the number of packets sent via LANE. If the count for packets to that destination exceeds a predefined threshold, the MPC is required to initiate the address resolution protocol to find the ATM address to be used for a direct connection to an egress MPC.

When a packet destined for a user who is outside the IASG (an inter-IASG packet) arrives at an ingress MPC, the latter sends a query to the route server that serves its IASG if the MPC wants to use a shortcut. In the spirit of NHRP, if the route server serves the target IASG, it will pass the query to the egress MPC (the target). The MPC will return its ATM address via the route server to the ingress MPC. Both the route server and the ingress MPC will cache the target's address, and the ingress MPC will establish a connection to the target address. If the route server does not serve the target IASG and does not have the address in its cache, it will forward the NHRP request to another route server that will use the same algorithm to find the target address. Figure 11.2 summarizes the operation of MPOA for inter-IASG traffic flows.

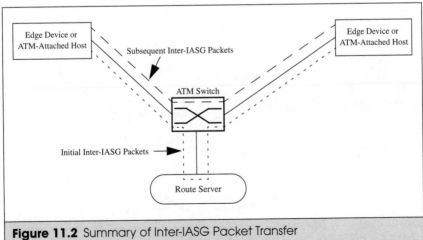

Figure 11.2 Summary of Inter-IASG Packet Transfer

11.4 Examples of MPOA Operation

Consider the ATM network in Figure 11.3. There are three IASGs (and hence three ELANs) defined in the network. ELAN C is associated with IASG 1; similarly, ELAN A is associated with IASG 2, and ELAN B is associated with IASG 3. There is one configuration server for both the LAN emulation service and the MPOA system. Each ELAN has an LES/BUS pair. There are two route servers; one serves IASGs 1 and 2, and the other serves IASGs 2 and 3. There are edge devices (ED) in each IASG as well as ATM-attached hosts (AHs). The edge devices are members of the ELANs. We have assumed that an edge device serves only one LAN emulation client (LEC); in Figure 11.3 the edge device assumes the role of a LEC.

11.4.1 Intra-IASG Flows

First, consider an intra-IASG traffic between a source behind ED1.1 and a destination behind ED1.2. Since both MPOA devices (ED1.1 and ED1.2) are in the same ELAN, the default LAN emulation operation can be used to handle the connection. During the discovery phase, ED1.1 and ED1.2 will have discovered that they both belong to the same ELAN. The flow diagram is identical to that used for LAN emulation (see Figure 9.3).

Assume that a packet originating from a user behind ED1.1 is destined for AH1.1. When ED1.1 receives the packet, if the edge device has a VCC to AH1.1 (a shortcut), it will send the packet over the short-

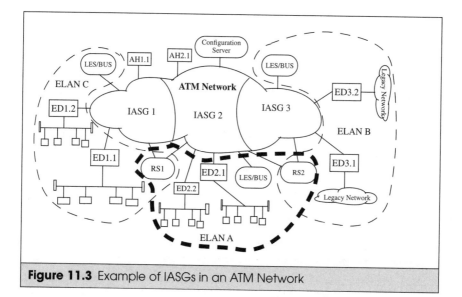

Figure 11.3 Example of IASGs in an ATM Network

cut. Otherwise, it will examine its cache entries for the ATM address of AH1.1. If there is no entry for AH1.1, ED1.1 has two options: use default forwarding for the packet or use shortcut forwarding.

- **Default Forwarding:** ED1.1 forwards the packet to the RS for its IASG (RS1) via the **RSend VCC**. Since RS1 is in the same IASG as AH1.1, it will forward the packet to the destination via the **RForward VCC**. While forwarding the packets to AH1.1 via RS1, ED1.1 keeps a count of all packets destined for AH1.1. If this number exceeds a threshold within a predefined time interval, ED1.1 will initiate an NHRP request for AH1.1's ATM address so it can establish a shortcut.
- **Shortcut Forwarding:** When ED1.1 receives a packet destined for AH1.1, it sends an NHRP request to RS1. On receiving the NHRP request, RS1 returns an NHRP response to ED1.1. Finally, ED1.1 then uses the address to establish a shortcut to AH1.1.

Figure 11.4 illustrates both situations.

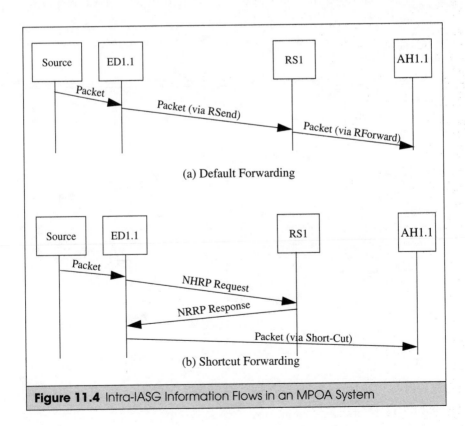

(a) Default Forwarding

(b) Shortcut Forwarding

Figure 11.4 Intra-IASG Information Flows in an MPOA System

11.4.2 Inter-IASG Flows

Consider a packet that arrives at ED1.1 in IASG1 and is destined for a user behind ED3.2 in IASG3. As before, if there is a shortcut to ED3.2, ED1.1 will send the packet via that shortcut. Similarly, if the ATM address of ED3.2 is cached, ED1.1 can establish a VCC to ED3.2. In the absence of these two options, ED1.1 can use either default forwarding or shortcut forwarding.

- **Default Forwarding:** Under this method, ED1.1 forwards the packet via LAN emulation to RS1. Since RS1 and RS2 are in the same ELAN, RS1 sends the packet to RS2 via LAN emulation. Since RS2 and ED3.2 are in the same ELAN, RS2 sends the packet to ED3.2 via LAN emulation.

- **Shortcut Forwarding:** Under this method, ED1.1 sends an NHRP request to RS1 (since RS1 is the NHS for its IASG) for the ATM address of ED3.2. RS1 forwards the request to RS2, which sends a cache imposition request to ED3.2. When RS2 receives a cache acknowledgment from ED3.2, it returns an NHRP response to RS1, and the latter forwards the response to ED1.1. Using the ATM address of ED3.2 that is contained in the NHRP response, ED1.1 establishes a VCC to ED3.2.

The flows for both default forwarding and shortcut forwarding are shown in Figure 11.5.

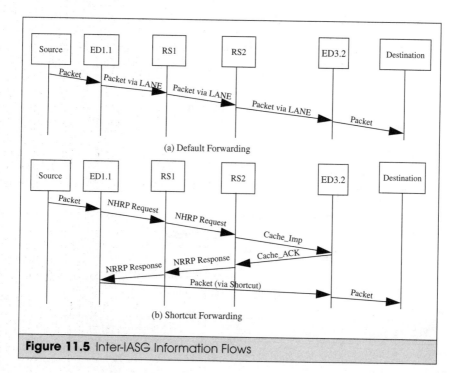

(a) Default Forwarding

(b) Shortcut Forwarding

Figure 11.5 Inter-IASG Information Flows

Note that in all the cases above the figure assumes that the edge devices and route servers will perform the appropriate encapsulation before a packet is forwarded. Our main goal in these examples is to highlight the information flow among the network entities.

11.5 The IP Switching Challenge

While the details of MPOA were being worked out, a new scheme, called **IP switching** (also known as **ATM under IP**) [72], was proposed. This scheme, together with several versions of it, has been implemented by different switch vendors. Before discussing IP switching, let us consider some of the negative comments that critics have made about ATM Forum's MPOA and IETF's IP over ATM schemes, including multiprotocol encapsulation over ATM [55] and classical IP over ATM [57]. These comments are essentially the motivations for developing IP switching.

First, MPOA and IETF's IP over ATM schemes implement both IP and ATM, each of which requires routing protocols. This leads to duplication of routing protocols and management and maintenance functions [73]. This, coupled with the fact that management functions are required to handle the interaction between the two routing protocols, is said to make it difficult to locate problems. Second, all currently proposed methods of routing IP over ATM have been accused of being too complex, thereby delaying their implementation. Third, the current proposed IP over ATM schemes make extensive use of route servers that are usually required to interconnect multiple logical subnets. In general, there is no autoconfiguration scheme that enables route servers to easily discover their neighbors. Consequently, there is often a great need to assign a route server's neighbors manually.

IP switching combines IP routing with ATM switching in a manner that attempts to minimize these problems. An IP switch consists of two major components: an **IP switch controller** and an **ATM switch**. The IP switch controller is essentially a router that is responsible for exchanging topology information with other IP switches. An IP switch routes the first packet in a transmission in a traditional store-and-forward manner. However, subsequent packets in a session can be sent in a circuit-switched manner over an ATM connection. This skips the routing function and consequently improves the throughput. Central to the IP switch operation is the ability to determine when to route and when to switch.

To do this, the concept of **flow** was introduced. A flow is a sequence of packets belonging to the same source-destination pair. The IP switch distinguishes between **short-lived flow** and **long-lived flow**. Short-lived flows are routed in a store-and-forward manner between IP routers using pre-established ATM connections between routers. Typical short-lived flows include Simple Network Management Protocol messages, Simple Mail Transfer messages, and name lookups. Long-lived

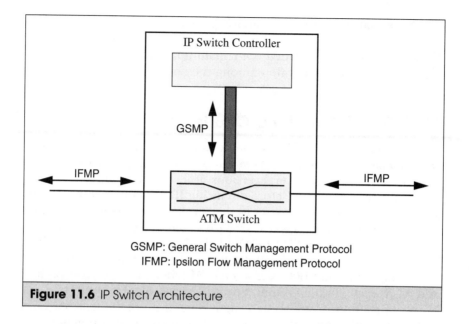

Figure 11.6 IP Switch Architecture

flows are mapped into an individual ATM connection; they are switched at layer 2 over an ATM network. Such flows include file transfers, Telnet sessions, Web downloads, and multimedia audio and video.

Two protocols are used to manage these flows. These are the **General Switch Management Protocol** (GSMP) [74] and the **Ipsilon Flow Management Protocol** (IFMP) [75]. GSMP is used within an IP by the switch controller to request the setup and tear down of ATM connections. IFMP is used between IP switches or between an IP switch and an edge device to associate flows with ATM connections. Figure 11.6 shows the architecture of the IP switch. The flow labelling produces what may be called a **connectionless ATM over IP** because the connections exist only on a node-by-node basis. As a result, a node or link failure only results in bypassing the affected links without the need to re-establish an entire end-to-end connection, as in traditional ATM operation.

11.5.1 IP Switch Detailed Operation

The default flow is the short-lived flow. Each IP node sets up a default virtual channel for forwarding IP traffic to the IP switch. When an IP node has new IP traffic to send to a downstream node, it forwards the first packet to the IP switch via the default virtual channel. An ATM input port in the IP switch forwards the packet to the IP switch controller for classification. The controller forwards the first packet in a traditional store-and-forward manner over a default ATM virtual channel while performing flow classification. If it is a short-lived flow, it does nothing. However, if it is a long-lived flow, it uses the GSMP to instruct the ATM switch to establish a virtual channel to the downstream IP node and uses the IFMP to advice the upstream IP node to send further packets of the flow over the new virtual channel. Figure 11.7 shows the operation of the switch.

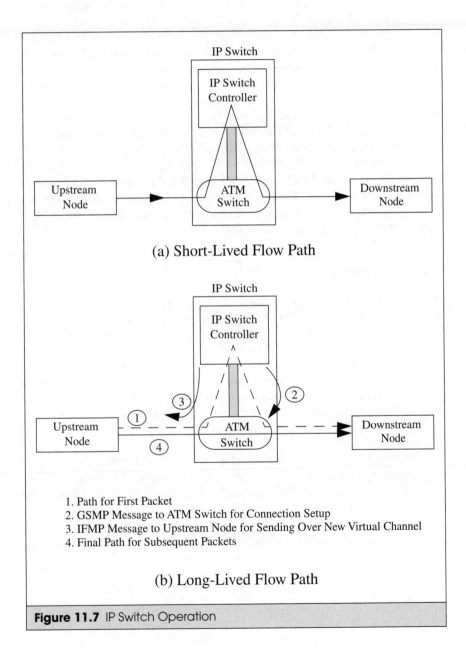

(a) Short-Lived Flow Path

1. Path for First Packet
2. GSMP Message to ATM Switch for Connection Setup
3. IFMP Message to Upstream Node for Sending Over New Virtual Channel
4. Final Path for Subsequent Packets

(b) Long-Lived Flow Path

Figure 11.7 IP Switch Operation

11.5.2 Comments on IP Switching

IP switching is a novel idea whose main weakness is the fact that it works only for IP and not for any other layer 3 protocol. However, since IP is the preeminent layer 3 protocol and essentially the *de facto* standard, such a limitation may not be a major handicap to the scheme.

Since the introduction of the Ipsilon IP switching concept, many types of layer 3 switching have been proposed. However, each of these schemes is essentially a variation on the Ipsilon theme. They differ mainly in the way they set up paths in the network. As stated above, the Ipsilon IP switching scheme is a **flow-based** scheme that uses flow classification (short-lived versus long-lived) to forward packets. While some of these newer proposals attempt to slightly modify the flow-based scheme, others are **topology-based** schemes that make forwarding decisions based on either the destination IP address or a combination of the source IP address and destination IP address [76]. The goal of this section is to introduce the reader to this new concept that poses a challenge to both the IETF IP over ATM and the ATM Forum multiprotocol over ATM schemes. Therefore, it is not our intention to discuss any of the contending proposals. The interested reader is referred to the different networking trade magazines.

11.6 Summary

MPOA is a service that provides end-to-end layer 3 connectivity across an ATM network. It is a service that is still being developed. The specification has undergone a number of revisions. The latest revision has drastically reduced the complexity of the MPOA protocols and simplified the operation of MPOA. MPOA can be considered an extension of the ATM LAN emulation, which is its default mode of operation. There is also the shortcut forwarding mode, in which an edge device or ATM-attached host chooses to establish a VCC to the destination prior to data transfer. This usually involves the need to use NHRP to perform address resolution.

IP switching is a new scheme that is posing a challenge to MPOA. IP switching classifies traffic into short-lived flows and long-lived flows. Short-lived flows are routed in a traditional store-and-forward manner while long-lived flows are sent in a circuit-switched manner over individual ATM connections. IP switching is one aspect of layer 3 switching that is becoming a product differentiator in the networking industry.

CHAPTER 12

Frame-Based Access Services

12.1 Introduction

Besides being the transport technology for LAN and IP traffic, ATM can also be the transport technology for many frame-based networks. These networks are characterized by the fact that they are based on the High Level Data Link Control (HDLC) protocol. These include frame relay [77, 78], **frame-based UNI** (FUNI) [79], and **ATM data exchange interface** (DXI) [80] networks. These services have a common frame format, as illustrated in Figure 12.1. However, the specifics of the header are different for frame relay networks and the other two.

FCS (frame check sequence) is a 16-bit field that is used for error detection and correction; frames with more than 4096 octets of user SDU may require a 32-bit FCS for adequate error detection.

12.2 ATM DXI

ATM DXI is a service that provides a standard procedure for interfacing legacy equipment such as a router to an ATM switch. ATM DXI prevents the legacy equipment from performing complex ATM functions

1 octet	2 octets	0–4096k octets (but up to 64k possible)	2 octets	1 octet
Flag	Header	User SDU	FCS	Flag

Figure 12.1 Frame Structure for DXI, FUNI, and Frame Relay Networks

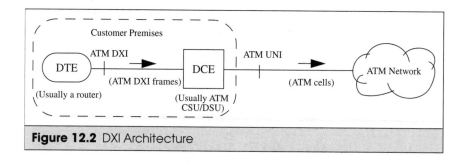

Figure 12.2 DXI Architecture

and shifts the burden to an ATM data service unit (DSU). The DSU then provides a UNI for the ATM network. It operates in three modes: mode 1a, mode 1b, and mode 2. The difference between modes 1a and 1b is mode 1a supports only AAL5 traffic while mode 1b allows at least one virtual connection to carry AAL3/4 traffic and others to carry AAL5. Similarly, the difference between mode 1 (a and b) and mode 2 is mode 1 allows up to 1023 virtual connections with 16-bit FCS while mode 2 allows up to 16,777,215 connections with 32-bit FCS. Figure 12.2 illustrates the operation of the ATM DXI.

As the figure illustrates, the DTE generates an SDU that is encapsulated into a DXI frame and passed to the DCE. The DCE then performs the AAL5 segmentation and reassembly function to generate the ATM cells. The cells are then forwarded to the ATM network over a T1 link.

The frame structure for DXI and FUNI is the same and is illustrated in Figure 12.3.

The different fields in the header are as follows:

- **Congestion notification** (CN): 1 bit. The DTE sets CN to zero. If the payload type identifier (PTI) is 01x (x = 0, or 1) in the last ATM cell composing the DXI frame (indicating a congestion condition), the DCE sets CN to 1 for that frame; otherwise it sets CN to 0.

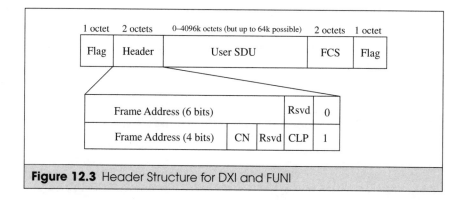

Figure 12.3 Header Structure for DXI and FUNI

- **Cell loss priority** (CLP): 1 bit. This field is the same as the CLP bit of the corresponding ATM cell header. It is copied into the header of its ATM cells.
- **Rsvd** is reserved and not used.

12.3 ATM FUNI

FUNI is based on the ATM DXI. It supports the three modes of operation defined for ATM DXI. The major differences between the FUNI and the DXI are in their access rates, the types of traffic they support, and where the cells are generated.

The ATM DXI supports only T1/E1 access from the customer's premises to the ATM network. FUNI supports fractional T1/E1 access as well as full T1/E1 access. FUNI provides a more efficient bandwidth utilization than ATM DXI. In addition, in FUNI, AAL3/4 is optional but in DXI, at least one virtual connection must be an AAL3/4. Finally, in FUNI, the SAR functions are performed in the ATM network; the traffic entering the ATM network consists of FUNI frames. This is illustrated in Figure 12.4.

FUNI also allows interoperability between ATM DXI and FUNI. It supports the switched virtual circuit. A FUNI source can make an SVC call to a FUNI, ATM DXI, or ATM UNI destination using the ATM UNI. However, FUNI supports only applications that use the AAL3/4 and AAL5 services; it does not support those that use the AAL1 service, such as circuit emulation service. The FUNI header is the same as the DXI header shown in Figure 12.3.

FUNI was developed to provide an ATM UNI in a frame format. There is a significant number of deployed equipment that is frame-based. This equipment can be software upgraded to be FUNI-capable. Compared to replacing these equipment or modifying them to have cell-based interfaces to the ATM network, the FUNI method represents significant cost savings.

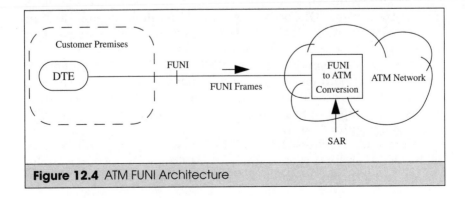

Figure 12.4 ATM FUNI Architecture

12.4 Frame Relay Over ATM

12.4.1 Overview of Frame Relay

Frame relay is a PVC-based data service, specified in the ITU-T Recommendations I.122 [77] and Q.922 [81], for interconnecting DTE devices across a public switched network. It is based on the core aspects of the LAPD (link access protocol D) protocol in which error detection is carried out in the network but no acknowledgment frames are exchanged between nodes in the network. If a frame is found to be in error, it is discarded; the retransmission is done by the end system. This reduces processing at the nodes and thus provides a higher speed than the X.25 network. Frame relay has no control fields and so has no frame types; it treats all frames alike as something to be delivered if possible.

Frame relay has a variable-length information field which, however, has a theoretical maximum of 4096 octets. It uses the **forward explicit congestion notification** (FECN) and the **backward explicit congestion notification** (BECN) bits to convey congestion conditions in the network. Specifically, when a switch experiences a congestion condition, it can set the FECN bit in frames travelling from the source to the destination so that the destination end system can notify the source end system to slow down. The BECN bit can be set in frames going toward the source to alert the source that its frames have encountered congestion. The source will then slow down. FECN is useful in those applications that practice destination-controlled flow control while BECN is useful in applications that practice source-controlled flow control. Note that the use of BECN assumes that traffic is flowing back to the source since the BECN is inside the user frame. When traffic is not flowing back to the source, a node that experiences congestion will generate a **consolidated link layer management message** that is sent to notify the source about the problem. A frame carrying this message is distinguished by the fact that it has a reserved data link connection identifier 1023.

The **data link connection identifier** (DLCI) identifies each virtual circuit within a shared physical channel. A frame relay switch maintains a table that identifies the various DLCIs and their associated user lines and interface trunk. DLCIs can have a local or global significance. In local DLCI addressing, DLCI values are significant only at one end of a frame relay virtual circuit. Thus, the same VC will be identified by different DLCIs at each end. In global DLCI addressing, a DLCI identifies the same VC at both ends; a switch does not translate the DLCIs in a packet as it does in the local DLCI addressing. While global DLCI addressing simplifies the address administration, it allows only 1024 DLCIs in the entire network.

An **extended address** (EA) bit is located at the end of each octet of the header. If an EA is set to 1, the current octet is the last octet of the header; and if the EA is set to 0, it is not. The most common implementation uses a 2-octet header. However, implementations exist that permit more than 2 octets of header; three and four octets are sometimes used. Only the 2-octet scheme is currently used on a D channel (i.e., the delta channel of the ISDN) in order to maintain compatibility with ISDN standards.

A **discard eligibility** (DE) bit is used to inform the frame relay network of the relative priority of frames. A frame with the DE bit set to 1 indicates to the network that the frame may be discarded before other frames if the network becomes congested. The more important frames have DE set to 0.

A **command/response** (C/R) bit is currently not used.

Frame relay can be provisioned in PVC or SVC mode. It uses a management protocol called local management interface (LMI). LMI frames have a unique DLCI address and are used to monitor the status of a link or PVC.

Figure 12.5 shows the frame structure for frame relay. The different fields are as follows:

- BECN (backward explicit congestion notification): 1 bit
- C/R (command/response): 1 bit
- DE (discard eligibility): 1 bit
- DLCI (data link connection identifier): 10 bits
- FECN (forward explicit congestion notification): 1 bit

Figure 12.6 shows header formats for 3-octet and 4-octet schemes. A 1-bit field called the **DLCI** or **DL-CORE control indication** (D/C) is used to indicate whether the remaining six bits of the DLCI are to be interpreted as DLCI bits or DL-CORE bits; the DL-CORE are used for the core services.

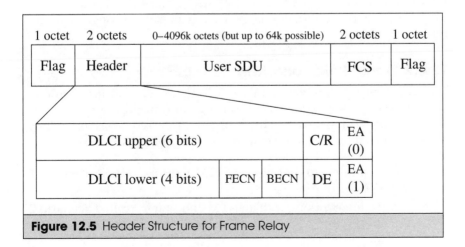

Figure 12.5 Header Structure for Frame Relay

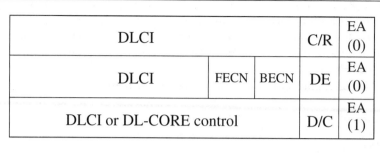

(a) 3-octet Header Format

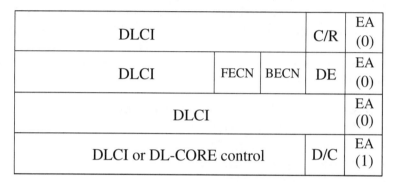

(b) 4-octet Header Format

Figure 12.6 Three and Four Octet Header Formats

An encapsulation method for carrying packets through a frame relay network is described in RFC 1490 [82]. The RFC also specifies a fragmentation procedure for large frames passing through a frame relay network with a smaller maximum frame size.

12.4.2 Frame Relay and ATM

The ITU-T in Recommendation I.555 [83] specifies an **interworking function** (IWF) that facilitates the transparent transport of frame relay service over ATM network. This is usually referred to as **tunneling**. There are two interworking scenarios defined in I.555 [84, 85]:

- Network interworking over an ATM network (called Scenario 1 in I.555)
- Service interworking with an ATM end system (called Scenario 2 in I.555)

Scenario 1 connects two frame relay devices using the ATM network while Scenario 2 connects a frame relay device with an ATM end system using the ATM network. In both of these scenarios, the IWF provides mapping and encapsulation functions necessary to ensure that the service provided to a frame relay device in not affected by the presence of the ATM transport. The two scenarios are illustrated in Figure 12.7.

The IWF for service interworking behaves like a protocol converter; it enables communication between dissimilar equipment. While the IWF for network interworking transports traffic transparently (since both source and destination end systems are frame relay devices), the IWF for service interworking does not transport traffic transparently. Note, however, that the ATM device at the other end has no knowledge that the device at this end is attached to a frame relay network. Because the service IWF is a "protocol converter," the user at

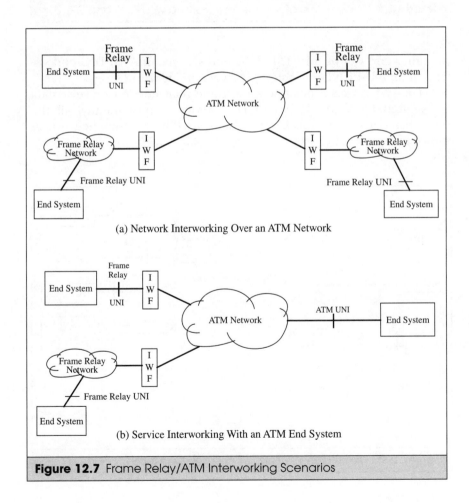

(a) Network Interworking Over an ATM Network

(b) Service Interworking With an ATM End System

Figure 12.7 Frame Relay/ATM Interworking Scenarios

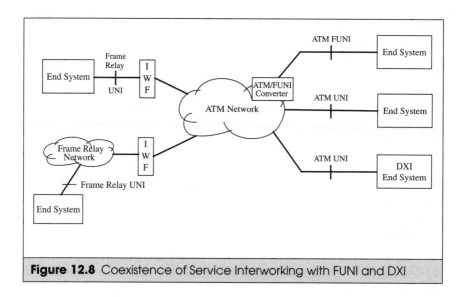

Figure 12.8 Coexistence of Service Interworking with FUNI and DXI

the other end can be an ATM FUNI end system, an ATM DXI system, or an ATM UNI end system, as shown in Figure 12.8.

The IWF makes it possible for a frame relay device to receive data transmitted by ATM FUNI and DXI devices. Consequently, all the frame-based access protocols can be supported in the same network, as shown in Figure 12.9.

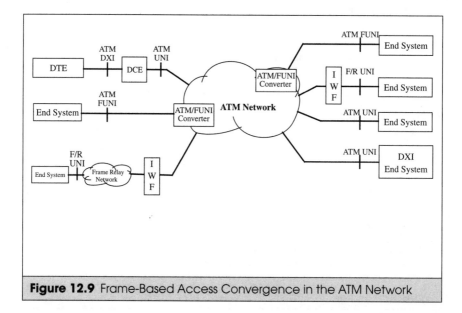

Figure 12.9 Frame-Based Access Convergence in the ATM Network

12.5 Summary

This chapter discussed the three frame-based access services. One advantage ATM DXI and FUNI have over frame relay over ATM is that DXI and FUNI do not have any need for the interworking function whose primary task is that of protocol conversion. They use the segmentation and reassembly functionality found in the ATM network. ATM DXI supports only T1/E1 rates while FUNI supports both full and fractional T1/E1 rates. As a result, FUNI provides better bandwidth utilization than DXI when the traffic is below the T1/E1 rate. ATM DXI involves a more complex set of operations in the customer premises to generate the ATM cells than FUNI which uses the ATM switch in the ATM network to provide the SAR function. All the frame-based access protocols can be supported in the same network. Further information on frame relay can be obtained from many books on the subject, such as [86].

CHAPTER 13

Audiovisual Multimedia Service

13.1 Introduction

The Digital Audio-Visual Council (DAVIC) defines digital audiovisual applications and services to be those applications and services in which there is a significant digital audio and video components [87]. These services include the following:

- **Movie-on-demand:** A network-delivered service that offers the functionality of home VCR.
- **Videoconferencing:** A real-time bidirectional service that permits the exchange of audio, video, and data information between multiple users located in two or more geographically separated sites.
- **Teleshopping:** A service that allows the user to browse video catalogs or virtual shops to purchase products and services.
- **Broadcasting:** A service that provides multiple users with immediate real-time access to multiple TV/radio/data programming.
- **Pay-per-view:** A specific broadcast that allows the user to view special TV programs without requiring a dedicated point-to-point connection to each user. Titles and start times are broadcast and the user selects a service at a designated time.
- **Delayed broadcast:** A service that allows the user to select a scheduled broadcast program to be stored at the network or service provider for delivery at a later time.
- **Distance learning:** A service that provides a "virtual classroom." The teacher and student are at different locations.

- **Videotelephony:** A service that allows two users at separate locations to initiate and control a conversation that may include the real-time bidirectional exchange of audio, video, and other data.

Other services include telecommuting, home banking, games, and telemedicine. Of these services, the ATM Forum has developed specifications for the video-on-demand service [88], which is the more popular name for movie-on-demand.

13.2 Video-on-Demand Service

Video-on-demand (VoD) provides the transfer of digitally compressed and encoded video information from a video server to a client [88]. At the destination, the stream is uncompressed, decoded, digital-to-analog converted, and presented at the client's monitor. VoD is an asymmetric service in which the bulk of the information flow is from the server to the client. The end user has a predetermined level of control on the selection of the material to be viewed as well as the time of viewing. VoD service provides end-to-end communication of video and audio information. The communication requires the synchronization of audio and video streams within the terminal. Figure 13.1 shows the VoD reference configuration.

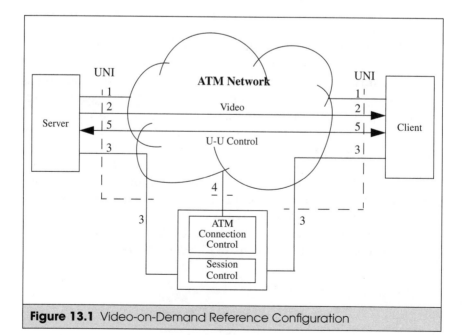

Figure 13.1 Video-on-Demand Reference Configuration

The interfaces are defined as follows:

- 1 is the UNI signaling interface for requesting the service. (That is, 1 is a control plane interface.)
- 2 is the principal information flow interface from the server to the client. (That is, 2 is a user plane interface.)
- 3 is the VoD session control information interface, a user plane interface.
- 4 is the ATM management plane interface in the case of PVC, and the proxy signaling ATM connection control in the case of SVC. It is a management plane interface in PVCs and control plane interface in SVCs.
- 5 is the user-to-user control information interface.

These interfaces separate information flows that are mapped as separate VCs on the physical UNIs at the interface to the network.

13.3 VoD System Structure

The VoD uses the MPEG-2 [89]. MPEG (Moving Pictures Expert Group) is a group of experts that generates standards for digital video and audio compression. The first standard, MPEG-1, defines a bit stream of compressed video and audio to fit a data rate of 1.5 Mbps but allows for data rates as high as 4.5 Mbps. The latest standard, MPEG-2, defines a bit stream of compressed video and audio for data rates of 2 to 10 Mbps. MPEG-2 offers a more efficient means to code interlaced video signals than MPEG-1.

VoD requires that the MPEG transport stream be constructed as a single program transport stream (SPTS). One SPTS is mapped into one ATM VC using the AAL5. The reason why AAL5 was chosen over AAL1, which is designed for the kind of CBR traffic that MPEG-2 generates, includes the fact that AAL5 is the most commonly available AAL and as a result, is cheaper to implement than other ATM adaptation layer types. Although AAL5 has no timing synchronization capability as AAL1 does, end-to-end timing relationships can be transmitted using the MPEG-2 timestamps and the AAL5 does not need to convey this information.

13.3.1 Network Adaptation

The MPEG-2 SPTS packets are required to be mapped into the AAL5 with a NULL Service Specific Convergence Sublayer. From 1 to N MPEG-2 transport stream (TS) packets are mapped into an AAL5 SDU. For SVCs, the value of N is established via ATM signaling 4.0 at call setup using the AAL5 Maximum CPCS-SDU negotiation procedure.

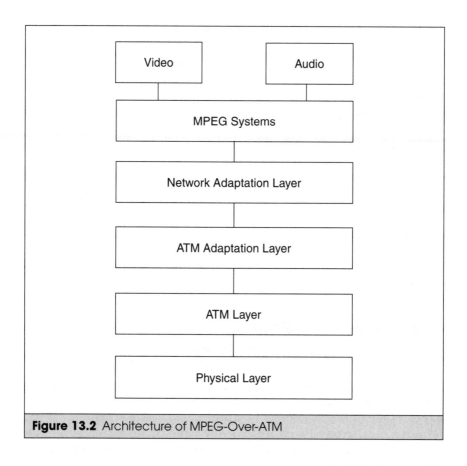

Figure 13.2 Architecture of MPEG-Over-ATM

The maximum CPCS-SDU size that can be signaled is N × 188 bytes, where N is the number of TS packets. For PVCs, the default value of N is 2. To ensure a base level of interoperability, every equipment must support N = 2, which gives the CPCS-SDU size of 376 bytes. With this network adaptation process, the architecture of an MPEG-over-ATM system becomes as shown in Figure 13.2.

Consider the simple base level where N = 2. An AAL5 SDU will contain two SPTS packets, each of which is 188 bytes (i.e., 376/2 bytes). To this CPCS-SDU, a CPCS-PDU trailer of 8 bytes is added, and this results in a 384-byte CPCS-PDU that maps into 8 ATM cells with no padding bytes. This situation is illustrated in Figure 13.3.

When a receiver receives a corrupted AAL5 CPCS-PDU that has a correct length field, it is advisable to pass the corrupted data, together with an indication that it is corrupted, from the adaptation layer to the demultiplexer layer rather than discarding the data in the adaptation layer. This is likely to improve system performance.

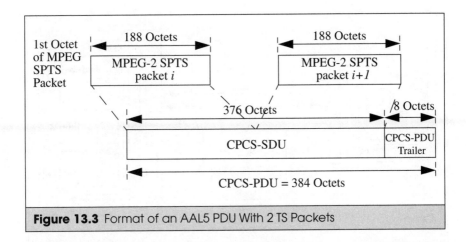

Figure 13.3 Format of an AAL5 PDU With 2 TS Packets

13.3.2 VoD Protocol Reference Model

Figure 13.4 shows the protocol reference model that applies to all the five interfaces shown in Figure 13.1. The control plane interfaces (1 and 4) support the Q.2931 protocols [19], the Q.2130 protocols (SSCF UNI) [90], and the Q.2110 protocols (SSCOP UNI) [20]. The user plane interfaces (2, 3, and 5) support H.222.0 protocols [89], the H.222.1

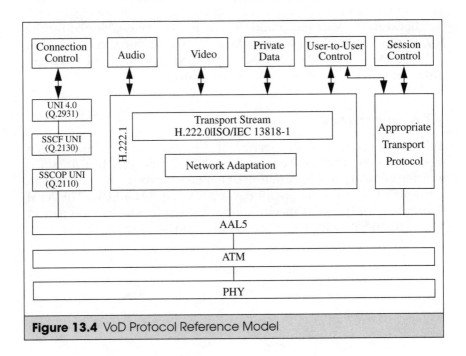

Figure 13.4 VoD Protocol Reference Model

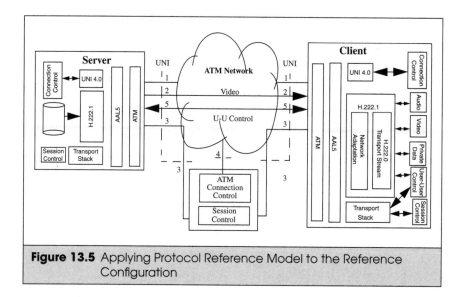

Figure 13.5 Applying Protocol Reference Model to the Reference Configuration

protocols [91], and appropriate transport protocols for session control and user-to-user control, such as the digital storage media command and control protocols [92] and the H.245 protocols [93].

When the VoD protocol reference model is applied to the reference configuration in Figure 13.1, we obtain the diagram in Figure 13.5.

Between the VoD server and the client, VCs are established for the U-U control and video (i.e., interfaces 2 and 5). These can be either SVCs or PVCs. SVCs are established via UNI signaling and PVCs are provisioned via management plane procedures.

13.4 Summary

This chapter presented an overview of the audiovisual multimedia service over ATM. The service uses the MPEG-2, and the data stream is transferred using AAL5. A network adaptation process is used to map many MPEG-2 transport stream packets into an AAL5 SDU. The ATM Forum has only issued a specification for the video-on-demand part of AMS. The specifications for other services will be issued in due course.

CHAPTER 14

Circuit Emulation Service

14.1 Introduction

ATM is essentially a packet-oriented transmission technology. In order to support CBR circuit-oriented traffic, ATM must emulate circuit characteristics. In particular, the performance realized over ATM for CBR traffic should be comparable to that obtained in current time-division multiplexing (TDM) technology. The ATM Forum has developed specifications for the **circuit emulation service** (CES) [94], and Figure 14.1 shows the ATM Forum CES reference model. There is a CES interworking function (IWF) between the ATM network and the CBR equipment. The role of the IWF is to extend the CBR circuit across the network transparently. The IWF monitors buffer overflows, cell loss, the absence of user traffic (or starvation condition), and the duration of the starvation.

Circuit emulation service uses AAL Type 1, and the AAL1 requirements depend on the type of CES that is being provided. The ATM Forum Circuit emulation can be classified into the following categories [94, 95]:

1. Structured DS1/E1 Nx64 kbps (Fractional DS1/E1) service
2. Unstructured DS1/E1 service
3. Unstructured DS3/E3 service

The unstructured DS3/E3 service is a new CES category that is defined in [95]. Since it is still under development, it will not be discussed in this chapter. Figure 14.2 shows the relationships of the protocol stacks at the IWF, the CBR equipment, and the ATM network.

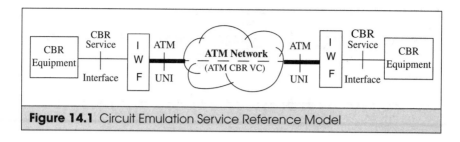

Figure 14.1 Circuit Emulation Service Reference Model

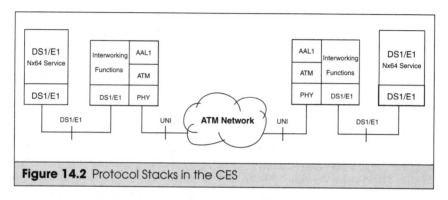

Figure 14.2 Protocol Stacks in the CES

14.2 Structured DS1/E1 Service

The structured DS1/E1 Nx64 service is modeled after the fractional DS1/E1 service and is intended to emulate it. In the case of DS1, N of the 24 slots in the frame are carried across the ATM network; the value of N can be anywhere from 1 to 24. For E1, N can take any value from 1 to 31. The service is useful in the following environments [94]:

- When there is a need to minimize ATM bandwidth by sending only time slots that are actually needed.
- When there is a need to provide clocking to the end-user equipment so that it fits into a fully synchronous network environment.
- When there is a need to provide accurate link quality monitoring and fault isolation for the DS1/E1 link between the IWF and the end-user equipment.

The Nx64 service can be divided into two groups:

1. Basic Nx64 service is used to support applications that do not require signaling or those that provide SS-7 signaling (i.e., N-ISDN).
2. Nx64 service with channel associated signaling (CAS) is used to support existing PBX and voice telephony equipment.

The Nx64 service with CAS requires the IWF to recognize and manipulate signaling bits (in the T1 frame), while the basic service does not require direct CAS support by the CES IWF. Every IWF is required to provide the basic service and may also provide the Nx64 service with CAS.

Since the Nx64 service uses only a fraction of the time slots available at the service interface, independent emulated circuits can share one service interface. In this case, the ATM layer is responsible for multiplexing and demultiplexing several VCCs, one for each AAL1 entity. Each AAL1 entity is responsible for performing segmentation and reassembly on one VCC, and a mapping function is responsible for assigning the stream input and output from the SAR process to specific time slots in the CES. This process is illustrated in Figure 14.3. A CES IWF providing Nx64 service is required to provide at least one AAL1 entity; it may provide multiple AAL1 entities, allowing several Nx64 connections to be multiplexed onto one service interface.

A significant source of delay in the Nx64 service is the amount of time it takes to collect enough data to fill a cell. This is called the **cell payload assembly delay**. This delay can be reduced by sending cells that are only partially full rather than waiting for the cell to be full. However, this reduction in delay comes with a reduction in cell rate. A CES IWF must be able to send cells without dummy octets, but may introduce dummy octets to complete the cell payload.

The IWF is required to detect several kinds of alarms. It may take one of many actions when an alarm is detected. The alarms include loss of signal (LOS), out of frame (OOF), remote alarm indication (RAI, also called "yellow"), and alarm indication signal (AIS). When an alarm

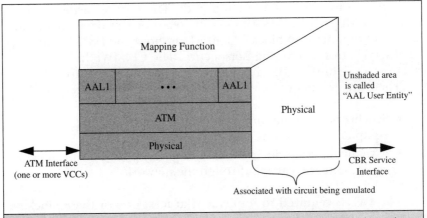

Figure 14.3 Structured DS1/E1 Service Interworking Function—Layering Perspective

is detected by the upstream IWF, it will use a **trunk conditioning** procedure to signal the alarm to the downstream DS1/E1 equipment. (Trunk conditioning is a technique used to make failed trunks appear busy so that they will not be seized until repairs have been made [96]. The busy condition is removed and the trunk is restored to service after repairs have been made.) The IWF will continue to emit cells at the nominal rate, but will set the DS1/E1 payload to an appropriate code to indicate Idle or Out-of-Service. Also, if signaling bits are being carried by the IWF, the upstream IWF will insert appropriate code into the DS1/E1 stream before segmentation takes place.

An Nx64 service IWF is required to provide a nominal timing at the DS1/E1 service interface. Several possible timing techniques are suggested in [94] and will not be discussed here.

14.3 Unstructured DS1/E1 Service

The unstructured DS1/E1 service is modeled after an asynchronous DS1/E1 circuit with repeaters. It is useful for the following environments [94]:

1. When non-standard framing is used by end-user DS1/E1 equipment.
2. When there is a need for a simple configuration of service. DS1/E1 has relatively few configuration options and so requires less knowledge of Telco practices.
3. When timing must be supported by end-user DS1/E1 equipment and carried through the network.

The unstructured DS1/E1 service covers those applications which utilize the entire DS1 (or E1) bandwidth. The service carries an arbitrary 1.544 Mbps (or 2.048 Mbps in the case of E1) data stream; the data is not organized in blocks. Figure 14.4 shows the DS1/E1 unstructured service from a layering perspective. The CES IWF has two physical layers, one for the CBR circuit to be emulated and one for ATM.

There are two modes for timing user equipment attached to the IWF:

- Synchronous mode, in which timing is supplied to the DS1/E1 equipment via the IWF service interface.
- Asynchronous mode, in which timing is supplied by the attached equipment and carried through the network.

The IWF is required to implement at least one of these clocking modes.

The unstructured service requires the IWF to fill the entire 47-octet cell payload with DS1/E1 data; no dummy payload octets are allowed.

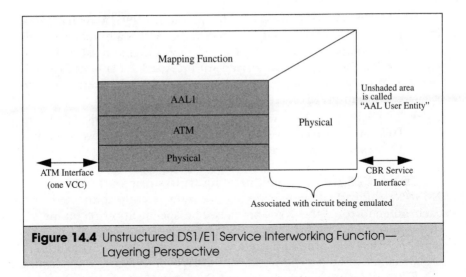

Figure 14.4 Unstructured DS1/E1 Service Interworking Function—
Layering Perspective

If lost cells are detected, dummy cells consisting of all 1s must be inserted when bit count integrity can be maintained. The receiving IWF will drop cells that the AAL header processor detects as misinserted.

14.4 CES Trunking for Narrowband Services

The two types of CES described previously handle broadband services. There is a need for support of narrowband services, especially voice and voiceband data. The ATM Forum has defined specifications for ATM trunking for narrowband services, the **voice and telephony over ATM** [97]. The specification extends the capabilities of CES to include the following capabilities:

- Efficient use of ATM for support of narrowband services (e.g., voice)
- Transport of compressed voice over ATM with optional voice activity detection

The goal is to specify how coded speech information can be mapped into ATM cells. Four methods have been identified for achieving this goal:

- Single-switched 64 kbps connection per VC, which is a call-by-call switch service that sets up an SVC for each individual voice call.
- The CES trunking method, which uses the Nx64 DS1/E1 service described earlier.

- The virtual trunk group (VTG) method, where a **virtual trunk group** is an ATM virtual connection that serves a number of CBR narrowband trunk circuits (i.e., Nx64 kbps channels). The narrowband channels are carried within AAL1 ATM cells over the VC in a manner that eliminates the need for echo control due to cell assembly/disassembly delays in voice calls.
- The hybrid method, which mixes the above methods. Here, the IWFs are connected with CES trunks or VTGs; the overflow traffic uses one-to-one switched connections.

In the CES trunking method, the trunks originating from the N-ISDNs (individual DS0 channels) are transparently connected with each other to form the Nx64 service. The specification recommends that individual links or groups of DS0 channels be mapped into individual VCs. The IWFs are connected via PVCs. Although individual users use signaling to access the network, the IWFs interfacing the network use PVCs across the network. One of the limitations of this scheme is that it requires all the IWFs to be fully meshed since no signaling-based routing is performed in the network between IWFs. This places a limit on the number of IWFs and hence on the number of N-ISDNs.

14.5 Summary

This chapter described the circuit emulation service (CES). There are two types of CES: structured Nx64 service and the unstructured service. The unstructured service is used by applications that utilize the entire DS1 or E1 bandwidth and the structured service is used for applications that employ fractional DS1 (or E1). CES uses an interworking function that performs a number of activities, including monitoring and measuring buffer overflows and cell loss. It compensates for cell loss and detects alarm conditions.

CHAPTER 15

ATM Inverse Multiplexing Service

15.1 Introduction

Modems have traditionally provided users access to the public network. However, modems are analog transmission devices. With the proliferation of digital switching and transmission technologies, it is now possible for digital lines to be used from the customer premises to the public switched digital network (PSDN). Several methods are used for access to the PSDN. These methods are usually defined in the form of dial-up access services which are offered by the telecommunications carriers. The most widely available dial-up services are the switched 56-kbps access service, T1 access service, and ISDN. Multirate ISDN service has recently been introduced [98, 99].

Many applications require transmission rates that are higher than 56 kbps but substantially less than T1. These applications are good candidates for the multirate ISDN access service. Unfortunately, the service is not widely available yet. An alternative access service is the fractional T1 service. In theory, the fractional T1 service is defined in incremental steps of 64 kbps in what is known as an Nx64-kbps service, where N = 1, 2, ..., 23. However, in practice, only a subset of these values of N is available. The user may have to pay for more bandwidth than he or she is actually using, thereby defeating the purpose of fractionalizing the T1. Inverse multiplexing is a method of aggregating channels that allows users greater freedom in selecting the optimum communication bandwidth and cost [100, 101].

15.2 Inverse Multiplexing Basics

Inverse multiplexing is a mechanism that permits multiple independent channels to be aggregated across a network to create one higher

173

rate channel. The aggregation process consists of individually dialing up the channels and combining them into a single data channel for a single data stream. An inverse multiplexer (or IMUX) is a device that implements inverse multiplexing.

Consider an application that requires 256 kbps data rate between two sites. This application cannot be supported on a DS0 channel at the rate of 64 kbps and will make an inefficient use of a T1 line at 1.544 Mbps. However, in the absence of a multirate ISDN service, this application can be supported on four DS0 channels by inverse multiplexing. An IMUX can dial up four DS0 channels through the public network and aggregate them into one 256 kbps channel. The inverse multiplexer segments the data that needs to be transmitted and sends it out over the individual channels. At the receiving end, another IMUX will combine the data from the four channels to reconstruct the original data stream. Figure 15.1 shows the inverse multiplexing architecture.

One of the fundamental issues in inverse multiplexing is synchronization. In the example in Figure 15.1, to get the data spread over the four channels, inverse multiplexing uses a cyclic round-robin scheme. The IMUX at the receiving end must ensure that the order the data streams are sent on the channels is the same order they are extracted so that the reconstructed stream is the exact replica of what was sent into the network, in the absence of any errors introduced by the channel. It must also compensate for the different delays between the channels, since the delay on some channels may be more than that on others.

Inverse multiplexing can dynamically add or subtract channels from an inverse-multiplexed connection without terminating the connection. In this way, the bandwidth of a connection between two endpoints exhibits the so-called **rubber bandwidth** feature [100]. Rubber bandwidth is the ability of the bandwidth between two endpoints to vary in accordance with the real-time requirements of the application. In the past many vendors implemented proprietary inverse multiplexing protocols. However, a consortium called the Bandwidth on Demand Interoperability Group (BONDING) has been formed to develop inverse multiplexing protocols that permit interoperability of equipment from different vendors.

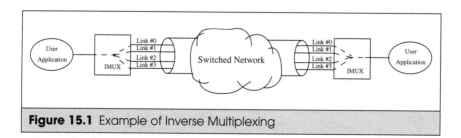

Figure 15.1 Example of Inverse Multiplexing

15.3 ATM Inverse Multiplexing

Access to ATM services is usually limited to the DS1/E1 rate because DS3/E3 links are not necessarily available throughout a given network. Inverse multiplexing for ATM (IMA) provides a way to combine transport bandwidths of multiple DS1/E1 links grouped to collectively provide higher intermediate rates [102]. Multiplexing of ATM cell streams is performed on a cell-by-cell basis across the links.

Figure 15.2 illustrates the IMA technique. IMA units are required at each end of the **link group**. At the source end, the ATM cell stream received from the ATM layer is distributed, on a cell-by-cell basis, across the multiple links within the link group. At the destination end, the IMA unit combines the cells from each link, on a cell-by-cell basis, to rebuild the original cell stream. Special cells that contain information that permits the reconstruction of the ATM cells at the destination IMA unit are transmitted periodically by the source IMA unit.

At the source end the cells are transmitted continuously; if there are no ATM cells, the IMA sends "filler" cells to maintain a continuous stream of cells at the physical layer. This keeps the IMA unit at the destination end in synch with that at the source end. If the two IMA units are not in synch, the reconstruction of the original stream at the destination end will be incorrect.

Inverse multiplexing is transparent to the application and the network since the cell order is maintained. Also, the required cell delay variation on each VC stays within the bounds negotiated at setup time. Consecutive cells on each link are grouped together to form an **IMA frame**. IMA frames play an important role in controlling the operation of the IMA.

15.4 IMA Unit Reference Model

Figure 15.3 shows the IMA unit reference model. It also identifies five functional components for IMA: source interface, cell function, IMUX, unit management, and link management.

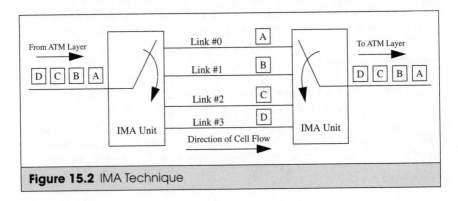

Figure 15.2 IMA Technique

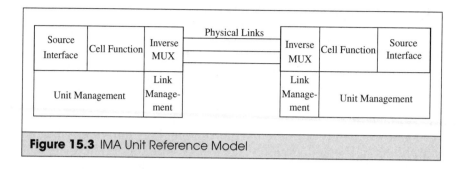

Figure 15.3 IMA Unit Reference Model

- The **source interface** provides the connection to an internal data bus (such as an ATM switch, router, or computer).
- The **cell function** is source interface dependent. If the source is directly connected to an ATM cell generating entity, then the cell function is null. If the source is a frame-based interface, such as DXI, the cell function provides frame-to-cell conversion.
- **Inverse multiplexing** provides the function of splitting and recombining cell streams.
- **Link management** is a function that provides direct management and establishment of the physical links. Link management is responsible for setting up, maintaining, and tearing down links.
- **Unit management** is a function that provides the management of all functions of the IMA. It provides an IMA MIB that allows IMA units to be monitored.

15.5 The IMA Control Protocol Cell

As stated earlier, a transmitting IMA distributes ATM cells coming from the ATM layer over N links in a cyclic round-robin manner on a cell-by-cell basis. The receiving IMA is responsible for accepting the cells from the N links, compensating for differential delays, rebuilding the original ATM cell stream, and passing the aggregate ATM cell stream to the ATM layer. The **IMA control protocol** (ICP) cells are used to maintain the coordination between the transmitting and the receiving IMA units.

The ICP cell is used by each IMA at the two ends to convey IMA configuration information to the other end of the IMA pipe. An ICP cell is sent every M cells on each link, where M can have values 32, 128, or 256. Thus, an **IMA frame** consists of M consecutive cells. The sending end staggers the ICP cells, giving them some offset in each link, where an offset of 0 means that the ICP cell is the first cell in the frame. Figure 15.4 shows the IMA frame concept. In this figure, the offset of the ICP cell on link #0 is 0, the offset on link #1 is 3, the offset on link #2 is 1, and the offset on link #3 is 2.

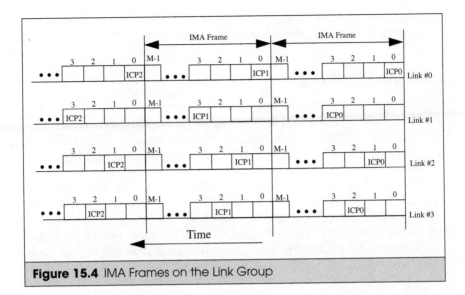

Figure 15.4 IMA Frames on the Link Group

15.6 Delay Compensation

Since cells travelling along different links may experience different amounts of delay, a mechanism must be established to compensate for the anticipated delay differences. Delay compensation uses the concept of IMA along with the ICP cell. As stated in the previous section, an IMA frame corresponds to M consecutive cells transmitted on a given link. ICP cells are sent one per link per IMA frame. The ICP cell can be located anywhere within the IMA frame; ICP cells should be spread out evenly across all links in the link group.

At the receiving end, each link delivers data into its own buffer that is deep enough to tolerate the maximum link delay variation. A receiving IMA unit has a read (or playback) pointer and a write pointer. The write pointer is used for receiving data from the network and storing it in the buffer. The read pointer is used for reading out data from the buffer for the reconstruction of the cell stream. Whenever a cell is written into a buffer, the write pointer is incremented. Similarly, when a cell is read out of the buffer, the read pointer is incremented. Until the first ICP cell is received, no cells are written into the buffer. Both pointers wrap around at the end of the buffer. Each cell received after the ICP cell is written into the buffer. The ICP cell contains the offset of the ICP cell in the IMA frame.

When the ICP cell is received, the pointer is initialized to the value of the ICP cell offset. The read pointers are aligned and cells are read out of the buffers in the assigned link multiplexing order. Adjustment of the write pointers provides the delay compensation. The differential delay between any two links is calculated from the difference between the write pointer values for the two links.

15.7 Cell Stuffing

Cell stuffing is a mechanism that is used to compensate for rate differences among the links in a link group. If some links are faster than others, the transmitting IMA unit may be forced to insert filler cells to prevent them from being idle. **Stuff cells** are sent periodically on the faster links.

A stuff cell is inserted immediately following the ICP cell within the selected IMA frame. The receiving IMA unit removes the stuff cells from the incoming cell stream. Stuff cells are distinguished by the **stuff indication code** in the preceding ICP cell. This code is used to show that if there is no stuff cell in this frame, there is a stuff cell in 1, 2, 3, or 4 IMA frames.

15.8 The Future of IMUX and IMA

Several new technologies are being developed that will have a serious impact on inverse multiplexing. One of them is the multirate ISDN, which was mentioned at the beginning of the chapter. When it is widely available, multirate ISDN may be preferred to inverse multiplexing because the user does not have to deal with the issue of synchronization and does not need to have more than one telephone number. However, the user may lose the ability to dynamically allocate the bandwidth; the rubber bandwidth feature may be lost.

15.8.1 ADSL vs. IMA

Another technology that seems to threaten inverse multiplexing is the asymmetric digital subscriber line (ADSL) [103]. While inverse multiplexing provides high data rates to the customer premises through channel aggregation, ADSL uses existing copper in the local loop to provide very high data rates. ADSL is currently in the trial stage; when it becomes widely available, it will reduce the need for inverse multiplexing.

ADSL transmits an asymmetric data stream, with much more coming downstream to the user (or subscriber) and much less going upstream to the network. This is in keeping with the fact that many broadband services are asymmetric: Video-on-demand, home shopping, and interactive multimedia access all feature high data rate demands downstream to the subscriber and relatively low data rate demands upstream. ADSL has a range of downstream data rates that depend on distance. Typical distance-rate associations are as follows:

18,000 feet	1.544 Mbps
16,000 feet	2.048 Mbps
12,000 feet	6.312 Mbps
9,000 feet	8.448 Mbps

Upstream rates range from 16 kbps to 640 kbps. In many countries, 18,000 feet covers virtually every subscriber; and even in those countries where it does not cover every subscriber, it covers more than half the subscribers.

Besides ADSL, there are other digital subscriber line technologies that are likely to have a major impact on inverse multiplexing. These include:

- **HDSL** (high-data-rate digital subscriber line) requires two twisted-pair lines and operates in a duplex mode at a rate of 1.544 Mbps upstream and 1.544 Mbps downstream. It is designed primarily for WAN and LAN access.

- **SDSL** (single-line digital subscriber line) requires a single twisted-pair line and is designed to operate on the existing copper wire between the Telco central office and the residence. It offers a data rate of 768 kbps upstream and 768 kbps downstream. It is designed for applications similar to those for HDSL. In addition, SDSL allows premises access for symmetric services. Neither HDSL nor SDSL supports voice communication without special customer equipment.

- **VDSL** (very-high-data-rate digital subscriber line), like ADSL, is asymmetric in its operation. It supports 13 Mbps to 52 Mbps data rates downstream and 1.5 Mbps to 2.3 Mbps data rates upstream. In addition to applications that can use ADSL, VDSL also supports HDTV. It covers a distance of 1,000 feet (for 52 Mbps) to 4,500 feet (for 13 Mbps) and requires the use of fiber optic cables.

ADSL is the most popular of these digital subscriber line technologies. The ADSL Forum has already released an ATM network architecture for ADSL called ATM Internet Model which is expected to support the services that are the targets for IMA. When the ATM Internet Model is implemented, the need for IMA will be greatly reduced.

15.9 Summary

This chapter presented an overview of the ATM Forum ATM inverse multiplexing. Inverse multiplexing is designed to permit higher access rates than are currently available via the T1/E1 links. It combines a set of links to form a link group and distributes ATM cells on the links in a cyclic round-robin manner at the source. They are combined at the destination to recreate the original cell stream. The process is transparent to both the user and the network. Control protocols have been developed to ensure synchronization between the sending and receiving IMA units. Also, delay compensation is used to account for expected differences in delay experienced in different links. Stuff cells are inserted to compensate for rate differences among the links in a link group. The reason for using stuff cells is to prevent the transmitting IMA from inserting filler cells on faster links to prevent them from being idle.

The impact of ADSL and other digital subscriber line technologies on ATM inverse multiplexing was also discussed. These technologies will reduce the need for ATM inverse multiplexing as they become more widely available.

APPENDIX A

Abbreviations

AAL ATM adaptation layer

ABR available bit rate

ACR allowed cell rate

ADSL asymmetric digital subscriber line

AFI authority format identifier

AH ATM-attached host

AIR additive increase rate

AIS alarm indication signal

AL alignment

AMS Audiovisual Multimedia Service

ANSI American National Standards Institute

ARP Address Resolution Protocol

ATM asynchronous transfer mode

ATMARP ATM Address Resolution Protocol

ATMF ATM Forum

B channel bearer channel

BAsize buffer allocation size

BECN backward explicit congestion notification

BICI Broadband Inter-Carrier Interface

B-ISDN broadband ISDN

BOM beginning of message

BONDING Bandwidth on Demand Interoperability Group

BRI basic rate interface

BRM backward RM

Btag beginning tag

BUS broadcast and unknown server

C/R command/response

CAC Connection Admission Control

CAS channel associated signaling

CBR constant bit rate

CCR current cell rate

CDV cell delay variation

CDVT cell delay variation tolerance

CER cell error ratio

CES circuit emulation service

CI congestion indication

CLIP calling line identification presentation

CLIR calling line identification restriction

CLP cell loss priority

CLR cell loss ratio

CMIP Common Management Information Protocol

CMR cell misinsertion rate

CN congestion notification

CNM Customer Network Management

CO Central Office

COM continuation of message

CP-AAL common part AAL

CPCS common part convergence sublayer

CPI common part identifier

CRC cyclic redundancy check

CS convergence sublayer

CS-PDU CS-protocol data unit

CS-SDU CS-service data unit

CSU channel service unit

CTD cell transfer delay

CTDV cell transfer delay variation

D/C DL-CORE control indication

D channel data (delta) channel

DAVIC Digital Audio-Visual Council

DCC Data Country Code

DCE data circuit-terminating equipment

DCE data communications equipment

DCF data communications function

DCN data communication network

DDI direct dialing in

DE discard eligibility

DFI domain format identifier

DLCI data link connection identifier

DLCI DL-CORE control indication

DQDB distributed queue dual bus

DSP domain specific part

DSU data service unit

DTE data terminal equipment

DTL designated transit list

DXI data exchange interface

EA extended address

ED edge device

EFCI explicit forward congestion indication

ELAN emulated LAN

EOM end of message

ER explicit rate

ESI end system identifier

Etag end tag

FCS frame check sequence

FDDI fiber distributed data interface

FDM frequency-division multiplexing

FEC forward error correction

FECN forward explicit congestion notification

FERF far-end receive failure

FRM forward RM

FRS frame relay service

FTP File Transfer Protocol

FUNI frame-based UNI

Gbps gigabits per second

GCRA Generic Cell Rate Algorithm

GFC generic flow control

GSMP General Switch Management Protocol

HDLC High Level Data Link Control

HDSL high-data-rate digital subscriber line

HEC Header Error Control

HO-DSP high-order DSP

IARP inverse ARP

IASG internetwork address subgroup

IASGID IASG identifier

ICD International Code Designator

ICP IMA Control Protocol

ICR initial cell rate

IDI initial domain identifier

IDP initial domain part

IE information element

IEEE Institute of Electrical and Electronics Engineers

IETF Internet Engineering Task Force

IFMP Ipsilon Flow Management Protocol

IISP Interim Inter-switch Signaling Protocol

ILMI integrated local management interface

IMA inverse multiplexing over ATM

IME interface management entity

IMUX inverse multiplexer

IP Internet Protocol

IPX internetwork packet exchange

IS integrated service

ISDN Integrated Services Digital Network

ISO International Standards Organization

ISUP ISDN user part

ITU International Telecommunications Union

IWF interworking function

Kbps kilobits per second

LAN local area network

LANE LAN emulation

LAPB Link Access Protocol — Balanced

LAPD Link Access Protocol D

LE_ARP LAN Emulation Address Resolution Protocol

LEC LAN emulation client

LEC ID LEC identifier

LECS LAN emulation configuration server

LES LAN emulation server

LGN logical group node

LI length indicator

LIS logical IP subnet

LLC Logical Link Control

LMI local management interface

LNS logical NBMA subnet

LOS loss of signal

M1 management interface 1

M2 management interface 2

M3 management interface 3

M4 management interface 4

M5 management interface 5

MAC media access control

MAN metropolitan area network

MARS Multicast Address Resolution Server

Mbps megabits per second

MBS maximum burst size

MCF message communications function

MCR minimum cell rate

MCS multicast server

MD mediation device

MF mediation function

MIB management information base

MID multiplexing identifier

MPC MPOA client

MPEG Moving Pictures Expert Group

MPOA multiprotocol over ATM

MPS MPOA server

MTP message transfer part

MTU maximum transfer unit

MUX multiplexer

N-ISDN narrowband ISDN

NBMA non-broadcast multi-access

NDIS Network Driver Interface Specification

NE network element

NEF network element function

NHRP Next Hop Resolution Protocol

NHS next hop server/NHRP server

NI no increase

NIST National Institute of Standards and Technology

NNI network-network interface

Nrm number of cells per resource management

nrt-VBR non-real-time variable bit rate

NSAP network service access point

NT1 network termination 1

NT2 network termination 2

OAM operations and maintenance

ODI Open Datalink Interface

OID object identifier

OOF out of frame

OPWA one pass with advertising

OS operations system

OSF operations system function

OSI Open Systems Interconnection

OUI organizationally unique identifier

PAD padding

PBX private branch exchange

PCI protocol control information

PCR peak call rate

PDU protocol data unit

PGL peer group leader

PID protocol identifier

PL pad length

PLCP Physical Layer Convergence Protocol

PMD physical medium dependent

PNNI private network-network interface

PRI primary rate interface

PRM protocol reference model

PSDN public switched digital network

PT payload type

PTI payload type identifier

PVC permanent virtual channel

PVC permanent virtual circuit

QA Q adapter

QAF Q-adapter function

QFC Quantum Flow Control

QoS quality of service

RAI remote alarm indication

RARP reverse ARP

RD routing domain

RDF rate decrease factor

RDI remote defect indication

RFC request for comment

RM resource management

RP reply

RPC remote procedure call

RQ request

RS route server

RSVP Resource Reservation Protocol

RTT round-trip time

rt-VBR real-time variable bit rate

SAAL signaling ATM adaptation layer

SAP service access point

SAR segmentation and reassembly sublayer

SCCP signaling connection control part

SCR sustainable cell rate

SDLC Synchronous Data Link Control

SDSL single-line digital subscriber line

SDU service data unit

SEAL simple and efficient adaptation layer

SEL selector

SMI structure of management information

SMTP Simple Mail Transfer Protocol

SN sequence number

SNAP Subnetwork Attachment Port

SNMP Simple Network Management Protocol

SNP sequence number protection

SPTS single program transport stream

SS7 Signaling System Number 7

SSCF service-specific coordination function

SSCOP Service-Specific Connection-Oriented Protocol

SSCS service-specific convergence sublayer

SSM single segment message

ST segment type

Stat Mux Statistical Multiplexing

SVC switched virtual channel

SVC switched virtual circuit

TA terminal adapter

TC transmission convergence

TCAP transaction capability application part

TCP Transmission Control Protocol

TDM time-division multiplexing

TE1 terminal equipment type 1

TE2 terminal equipment type 2

TFTP Trivial File Transfer Protocol

TMN Telecommunications Management Network

TS transport stream

TSAP transport service access point

UBR unspecified bit rate

UDP User Datagram Protocol

UNI user-network interface

UPC Usage Parameter Control

UU user-to-user indication

VBR variable bit rate

VC virtual channel

VCC virtual channel connection

VCI virtual channel identifier

VCL virtual channel link

VDSL very-high-data-rate digital subscriber line

VLAN virtual LAN

VoD video on demand

VP virtual path

VPC virtual path connection

VPI virtual path identifier

VPL virtual path link

VTG virtual trunk group

WAN wide area network

WS workstation

WSF workstation function

Glossary

AAL (ATM Adaptation Layer) – The layer in the broadband integrated services digital network (B-ISDN) protocol hierarchy that adapts user traffic to a cell format.

AAL1 (ATM Adaptation Layer Type 1) – A protocol standard used for transporting constant bit rate (CBR) traffic and for emulating DS-1 and E-1 systems.

AAL2 (ATM Adaptation Layer Type 2) – A protocol standard used for transporting real-time variable bit rate (VBR) traffic, such as packetized audio and video.

AAL3/4 (ATM Adaptation Layer Types 3 and 4) – A protocol standard used for supporting both connectionless and connection-oriented VBR traffic.

AAL5 (ATM Adaptation Layer Type 5) – A protocol standard used for supporting connectionless VBR traffic, such as local area network (LAN) traffic.

ABR (Available Bit Rate) – A type of service where the network guarantees only a minimum cell rate (MCR) and adapts any rate higher than the MCR to the conditions of the network.

ACR (Allowed Cell Rate) – The rate at which an ABR user may transmit in the network.

Addressing – A mechanism by which end systems attached to a network can be uniquely identified.

AFI (Authority and Format Identifier) – A part of the network level address header that identifies the network addressing authority that is responsible for allocating values to the initial domain identifier (IDI).

AIS (Alarm Indication Signal) – An operations and maintenance (OAM) message that is sent to inform a downstream node that a fault has been detected upstream in a network element that supports a virtual channel connection (VCC) that passes through the node.

AMS (Audiovisual Multimedia Service) – A service specified by the ATM Forum for transmitting video-on-demand (VoD) over the ATM network.

ANSI (American National Standards Institute) – An organization that defines U.S. standards for the information processing industry.

ARP (Address Resolution Protocol) – A protocol specified in RFC 826 which binds a media access control (MAC) address to an Internet Protocol (IP) address.

Asynchronous Communication – A method of transmitting data in which each transmitted character is sent separately.

ATM (Asynchronous Transfer Mode) – The transfer mode for B-ISDN in which information is organized in fixed-size units called cells.

ATMARP (ATM Address Resolution Protocol) – An address resolution protocol defined in RFC 1577 for Classical IP over ATM.

ATMARP Server – A physical device associated with a logical IP subnet (LIS) that provides directory services functions to the hosts in the LIS.

ATMF (ATM Forum) – An industry alliance of vendors and telecommunications companies that makes recommendations and produces specifications for ATM networks and services.

ATM Traffic Descriptors – A generic list of traffic parameters that be used to characterize a requested ATM connection.

B-Channel (Bearer Channel) – A circuit-switched digital channel that can carry data, voice, and video signals at speeds up to 64 kbps.

B-ISDN (Broadband Integrated Services Digital Network) – An ITU-defined service that uses ATM as the switching scheme and provides support for integrated high-speed transmission of voice, video, and data in a uniform manner in the same network.

BECN (Backward Explicit Congestion Notification) – A resource management (RM) cell type generated by the network to indicate congestion or near-congestion condition for the traffic in the direction opposite to that of the BECN cell.

Best Effort – A quality of service (QoS) class in which no specific traffic parameters and no guarantees are provided; best effort usually refers to the unspecified bit rate (UBR) traffic.

B-ICI (Broadband Inter-Carrier Interface) – ATM Forum defined specification for the interface between public ATM networks to support user service connections across multiple public ATM networks.

BRI (Basic Rate Interface) – An ISDN service that provides two bearer 64-kbps channels (B-channels) and one 16-bit data channel (D-channel). It is also known as the "2B + D" service.

BRM Cell (Backward Resource Management Cell) – An RM cell that has been turned around by the destination end system.

Broadcast – A transmission destined for all users in a network.

Burstiness – The ratio of the peak cell rate (PCR) to the average cell rate.

BUS (Broadcast and Unknown Server) – A server in an emulated LAN (ELAN) that handles all multicast and broadcast traffic as well as initial unicast frames sent before a LAN emulation client-to-LAN emulation client (LEC-to-LEC) connection is established.

CAC (Connection Admission Control) – A set of actions taken by the network during a call setup phase to determine whether the call can be admitted or rejected.

CBR (Constant Bit Rate) – An ATM service category that supports the transmission of a continuous bit stream of traffic from those applications, such as video, voice, and circuit emulation, which require rigorous timing control and performance parameters.

CCR (Current Cell Rate) – An RM-cell field set by the source to its current allowed cell rate (ACR) when it generates a forward RM cell.

Cell – The basic unit of transmission in an ATM network. It is a fixed-size packet of 53 bytes: 48 bytes of payload and 5 bytes of header.

Cell Tagging – A technique used to distinguish between conforming cells and non-conforming cells. Non-conforming cells are tagged and can be dropped in the network when congestion is experienced.

CES (Circuit Emulation Service) – An ATM Forum service that supports the emulation of existing time-division multiplexing (TDM) circuits over ATM networks.

CI (Congestion Indication) – A condition carried in a 1-bit field in the resource management cell. CI is used to cause the source to decrease its ACR using a predefined algorithm.

Circuit Switching – A transmission technique in which a physical circuit is established between the sender and the receiver before transmission can take place.

CLP (Cell Loss Priority) – A bit in the ATM cell header that indicates two levels of priority in the ATM cell. CLP = 0 cells have a higher priority than CLP = 1 cells.

CLR (Cell Loss Ratio) – A QoS parameter that gives the ratio of the lost cells to the total number of transmitted cells.

Cluster – A group of hosts in an IP network that are served by a multicast address resolution server (MARS).

CMIP (Common Management Information Protocol) – An ITU-T management standard that can support operations, administration, maintenance, and provisioning functions.

Connection-oriented – A service in which a data path is established before data packets can be exchanged between the source and the destination.

Connectionless – A service in which data packets are sent into the network without prior connection setup; a packet has a destination address, and the network delivers it on a best-effort basis.

CPCS (Common Part Convergence Sublayer) – Part of the AAL convergence sublayer (CS) that must be present in all AAL implementations.

CPI (Common Part Indicator) – A 1-byte field in the CPCS-PDU in AAL3/4 that indicates the counting units used in the BASize and Length fields of the protocol data unit (PDU). (Currently only CPI = 0, units in bytes, has been defined.)

Crankback – A private network-network (PNNI) mechanism for partially releasing a connection setup in progress which has encountered a partial failure. Crankback allows the PNNI to perform alternate routing.

CRC (Cyclic Redundancy Check) – A set of error-detecting checksums used in data communications.

CS (Convergence Sublayer) – The upper half of the AAL where non-ATM formats (such as frame relay) are converted to ATM formats.

CSU (Channel Service Unit) – Equipment used at the user end that provides an interface between the user and the telecommunications carrier's network. In the past, the CSU was a separate unit from the data service unit (DSU) and was located where the Telco line entered the customer's premises or at the Telco's wiring closet. However, now it is not uncommon for the CSU to be integrated with the DSU as a single device that goes by the name DSU/CSU.

CTD (Cell Transfer Delay) – The time it takes for a cell to be transferred from its source to its destination over a given virtual channel (VC).

CTDV (Cell Transfer Delay Variation) – A parameter used to bound the randomness introduced in inter-cell spacing (and hence in the CTD) by the multiplexing process at a switch.

D Channel (Data (or delta) Channel) – A circuit-switched digital channel used for signaling in N-ISDN and which may optionally be used for packet data transmission. A D-channel can support data speeds of up to 16 kbps in basic rate interface ISDN and 64 kbps in primary rate interface ISDN.

DCC (Data Country Code) – A 2-byte field in a network service access point (NSAP) address that specifies the country in which the address is registered.

DCE (Data Circuit-Terminating Equipment or Data Communications Equipment) – A generic name for equipment that connects a DTE to the network; for example, a modem.

DLCI (Data Link Connection Identifier) – The address field in a frame relay frame.

DQDB (Distributed Queue Dual Bus) – A metropolitan area network technology defined in IEEE 802.6. It uses two buses that carry data in opposite directions and each station in the network connects to both buses.

DS-*n* (Digital Signal, Level n) – Physical interface for digital transmission at the rate of 64 kbps for DS-0 (i.e., $n = 0$), 1.544 Mbps for DS-1 (i.e., $n = 1$), 6.312 Mbps for DS-2 (i.e., $n = 2$), 44.736 Mbps for DS-3 (i.e., $n = 3$), and 274.176 Mbps for DS-4 (i.e., $n = 4$).

DSP (Domain Specific Part) – The part of an NSAP address that contains the address determined by the network authority.

DSU (Data Service Unit) – Equipment at the user end which acts as a telephony-based interface between low-rate services and higher rate circuits. It translates the digital signal coming from a data terminal equipment (DTE) into a digital signal that is appropriate for transmission over the carrier's network. In the past, the DSU was a separate unit from the CSU and was located next to the DTE. However, now it is not uncommon for it to be integrated with the CSU as a single device that goes by the name DSU/CSU.

DTE (Data Terminal Equipment) – The generic name for devices, such as workstations, that provide the end user with access to the network.

DTL (Designated Transit List) – A list of nodes that completely specifies a path from the source to the destination in a PNNI environment.

DXI (Data Exchange Interface) – An ATM Forum frame-based ATM interface defined between a DTE and a DCE.

E-*n* (European Digital Signal n) – European standard for digital interfaces at 2.048 Mbps (for *n* = 1), at 34.368 Mbps (for *n* = 3), and at 139.268 Mbps (for *n* = 4).

EFCI (Explicit Forward Congestion Indication) – A 1-bit field in the PTI that contains information on whether a transit node is congested or not.

E-LAN (Emulated LAN) – A logical network initiated by using the mechanisms defined by the ATM LAN Emulation.

ER (Explicit Rate) – A field in the resource management cell that indicates the cell rate that the source should use over the VC.

ESI (End System Identifier) – A 6-byte field that is used to uniquely identify an end system within an area. The ESI is usually the IEEE 802 MAC address.

FCS (Frame Check Sequence) – A mathematical formula that derives a numeric value based on the bit pattern of a transmitted block of data and uses that value at the destination to determine the existence of any errors that may have been introduced along the path.

FDDI (Fiber Distributed Data Interface) – An optical fiber token-passing ring LAN with dual counter-rotating rings.

FDM (Frequency-Division Multiplexing) – See **Multiplexing**.

FEC (Forward Error Correction) – A technique used to detect and correct errors in a digital data stream so as to avoid retransmissions.

FECN (Forward Explicit Congestion Notification) – A bit in a frame relay frame which when set, indicates to the destination end system that somewhere along the path, the current frame encountered a congested node.

FERF (Far-End Receive Failure) – An operations and maintenance (OAM) message that is sent to inform an upstream node that a fault has been detected downstream in a network element that supports a virtual channel connection (VCC) that passes through the node.

Fractional T1 – A service offered by network service providers. It supports data rates between 64 kbps (or DS0 rate) and 1.536 Mbps (or DS1 rate) and specified in multiples of 64 kbps.

FRM Cell (Forward Resource Management Cell) – An RM cell that is travelling from the source to the destination.

FRS (Frame Relay Service) – A connection-oriented, frame-based data service that can carry up to 4096 bytes of information per frame.

FUNI (Frame-based UNI) – An ATM Forum frame-based ATM interface defined between the end system and the ATM network.

GCRA (Generic Cell Rate Algorithm) – A model proposed by the ATM Forum that is used to define conformance with respect to the traffic contract of the connection.

GFC (Generic Flow Control) – A field in the ATM cell header that can be used to provide local functions, such as local flow control.

HDLC (High Level Data Link Control) – An ITU data link layer protocol standard for point-to-point and point-to-multipoint communication that performs hop-by-hop error checking and flow control.

Header – The protocol control information located at the beginning of a PDU.

HEC (Header Error Control) – A 1-byte field in the cell header used for detecting and correcting errors that may occur in the contents of the cell header.

Hello Packet – A type of PNNI routing packet exchanged between neighboring logical nodes.

IARP (Inverse ARP) – A protocol specified in RFC 1293 which enables the ATMARP server to obtain the ATM address of the host that requested an IP address to ATM address resolution.

IASG (Internetwork Address Subgroup) – A range of internetwork layer addresses summarized into an internetwork layer routing protocol.

ICD (International Code Designator) – A 2-byte field in the NSAP address that specifies an international organization. The codes for this field are defined by the British Standards Institute.

ICR (Initial Cell Rate) – A parameter associated with ABR service that defines the rate, in cells/second, at which a source should send data initially and after an idle period.

IDI (Initial Domain Identifier) – A 2-byte field in the NSAP address that specifies the addressing domain and network addressing authority which is responsible for allocating the values of the DSP.

IDP (Initial Domain Part) – A three-byte field in the NSAP address that contains the AFI and the IDI.

IEEE (Institute of Electrical and Electronics Engineers) – An international professional organization that has been responsible for many networking standards, including standards for LANs and MANs.

IETF (Internet Engineering Task Force) – An organization that is responsible for developing standards and specifications for TCP/IP networking.

IISP (Interim Inter-switch Signaling Protocol) – The predecessor of the PNNI (also referred as PNNI Version 0) that is not as sophisticated as PNNI Version 1.0. It was intended to be used on an interim basis until the completion of the PNNI Version 1.0 specification.

ILMI (Integrated Local Management Interface) – An ATM Forum-defined SNMP-based network management system that performs configuration, fault, and performance management functions between an end user and a private or public ATM network as well as between a private ATM network and a public ATM network.

IMA (Inverse Multiplexing over ATM) – A service that allows multiple T-1 or E-1 links to be combined into a single link group that provides a broadband facility for the transmission of ATM cells.

IME (Interface Management Entity) – Software at the user-network interface (UNI) that provides the ILMI functions.

IMUX (Inverse MUX) – A device that demultiplexes a single data stream into many output streams.

Internet – The world's largest internetwork that connects thousands of networks around the world.

Internetwork – A collection of networks interconnected to act as a single network.

Inverse Multiplexing – A process that combines several lower bandwidth circuits into one logical circuit of greater bandwidth to be used by a single data stream.

IP (Internet Protocol) – A network layer protocol defined in RFC 791 that provides connectionless service to the higher layer transport protocol. IP contains addressing and control information that enables packets to be routed.

IP Address – A unique 32-bit number assigned to a host that is attached to a TCP/IP network. The address is written as four decimal numbers, each between 0 and 255, separated by periods. Each decimal number in this "dotted decimal" format is the value of the corresponding byte in the IP address. For example, 140.156.32.21 is a valid IP address.

IP Switching – A switching scheme which integrates IP routing and ATM switching. It classifies traffic into two types of flows: short-lived flows and long-lived flows. Short-lived flows are handled by traditional IP routing. Long-lived flows are handled by ATM switching after the first packet in the flow has been handled by IP routing.

IPX (Internetwork Packet Exchange) – The network layer protocol for the Novell Netware.

ISDN (Integrated Services Digital Network) – A technology that permits a mix of traffic types (voice and data) to be offered in an all-digital network with standard interfaces for user access.

ISO (International Standards Organization) – A Geneva-based international organization that establishes voluntary standards for its member countries.

ITU (International Telecommunications Union) – An international organization which defines recommendations and standards relating to the international telecommunications industry.

LAN (Local Area Network) – A private network that provides high-speed data transfer over a short distance, usually spanning a building or a campus.

LANE (LAN emulation) – A service defined by the ATM Forum that uses an ATM network as a backbone for interconnecting legacy LANs and ATM-attached end systems.

LE_ARP (LAN emulation ARP) – A message sent by a LAN emulation client (LEC) to a LAN emulation server (LES) to solicit a mapping from a MAC address to ATM address.

Leaky-Bucket Algorithm – A flow control algorithm that monitors cells to see if they conform to the traffic contract for that VCC. Non-conforming cells are either tagged or dropped from the network.

LEC (LAN Emulation Client) – An entity in an ATM end system that performs data forwarding and address resolution in an ELAN.

LECS (LAN Emulation Configuration Server) – A server that provides configuration information to LECs, thereby assigning them to ELANs.

LES (LAN Emulation Server) – An entity that provides control functions in LANE by enabling LECs to join an ELAN and resolving MAC addresses to ATM addresses.

LGN (Logical Group Node) – A single node that represents the lowest level peer groups in the respective higher level peer groups.

LIS (Logical IP Subnet) – A group of IP nodes which are served by one ATMARP server in an ATM network.

Loopback – A diagnostic test in which the transmitted packet or cell is returned to the sending device after passing through a predefined segment of a network.

M1 (Management Interface 1) – The interface for managing ATM end devices.

M2 (Management Interface 2) – The interface for managing private ATM networks or switches.

M3 (Management Interface 1) – The interface for managing the links between private and public networks.

M4 (Management Interface 4) – The interface for managing public ATM networks.

M5 (Management Interface 5) – The interface for managing the links between two public ATM networks.

MAC (Media Access Control) – An IEEE specification for the lower part of the data link layer (layer 2) which determines how a device transmits packets in an IEEE 802 LAN.

MAC Address – A 6-byte unique identification code used by the MAC layer to identify devices on a network. It consists of two parts: a manufacturer's identification number and a sequential identification number. MAC addresses are written in hexadecimal format with the hex value of each byte separated from that of the next byte by a hyphen. For example, 00-80-1D-0E-44-4C is a valid MAC address.

MAC Layer – The lower sublayer of the data link layer of the open systems interconnection (OSI) reference model.

Managed Object – A network device that can be managed by a network management protocol.

MARS (Multicast Address Resolution Server) – A device proposed as an extension of the RFC 1577 model to facilitate the handling of IP multicasting in an ATM network.

MBS (Maximum Burst Size) – A traffic parameter that specifies the maximum number of cells that can be transmitted at the peak rate (PCR) and still be in conformance with the GCRA.

MCR (Minimum Cell Rate) – An ABR service traffic parameter that determines the rate, in cells/second, that a source is always allowed to send.

MCS (Multicast Server) – A device proposed as an extension of the MARS model which is responsible for establishing point-to-multipoint VCs. Each host in the multicast group forwards all multicast packets to the MCS, and the MCS is responsible for delivering the packets to the members of the group.

MIB (Management Information Base) – A collection of management objects for a network component that can be accessed via a network management protocol. MIB-I, documented in RFC 1156, is defined for managing TCP/IP networks. MIB-II, documented in RFC 1213, is an extension of MIB-I; it is the current standard MIB for TCP/IP networks.

MPC (MPOA Client) – A protocol entity that implements the client side of the multiprotocol over ATM (MPOA) protocol.

MPEG (Motion Picture Expert Group) – An ISO group that establishes standards for video and audio compression techniques and mechanisms for multiplexing and synchronizing various media streams.

MPEG-1 – An ISO standard for decoding video of moderate resolution resulting in bit rates of about 1.5 Mbps.

MPEG-2 – An ISO standard for decoding video of high resolution which results in bit rates of 1.5 Mbps to 10 Mbps.

MPOA (Multiprotocol over ATM) – An ATM Forum specified service that permits layer 3 protocols, such as IP, to be transported over the ATM network.

MPOA Service Area – A collection of physical devices consisting of an MPOA server and the set of clients served by that server.

MPS (MPOA Server) – A protocol entity that implements the server side of the MPOA protocol.

Multicast – A transmission that is destined for a predefined group of users in a network.

Multiplexing – The process of combining a number of individual channels into one channel. Multiplexing can be done in the frequency domain to yield frequency-division multiplexing (FDM). It can also be done in the time domain to yield time-division multiplexing (TDM).

MUX (Multiplexer) – A network device that combines many input data streams into one single stream for transmission over a shared physical medium.

N-ISDN (Narrowband ISDN) – The original ISDN, as opposed to broadband ISDN.

NBMA Network (Non-broadcast Multi-access Network) – A network that allows multiple hosts to be attached to it but does not permit the use of broadcasting as in LANs. Examples of NBMA networks include X.25 and ATM networks.

NDIS (Network Driver Interface Specification) – An interface specification developed by Microsoft to separate communication protocols from personal computer networking hardware.

NHRP (Next Hop Resolution Protocol) – A protocol proposed to be used for address resolution in the classical IP network.

NHS (NHRP Server) – A device in an NBMA network that serves the hosts in a logical NBMA subnet.

NI (No Increase) – A 1-bit field in the resource management cell that is used to prevent the source from increasing its ACR.

NNI (Network-Network Interface) – ITU-specified interface between two nodes (switches) in the same network. The ATM Forum distinguishes between the private NNI (PNNI) for private networks and the public NNI.

NSAP (Network Service Access Point) – The point at which an OSI network service is made available to a Transport layer entity.

NT1 (Network Termination 1) – A functional group, defined for N-ISDN, that represents the termination of the physical connection between the customer site and the local exchange.

NT2 (Network Termination 2) – A functional group, defined for N-ISDN, that provides local switching and multiplexing service, such as a PBX.

OAM (Operations and Maintenance) – A set of network management functions that provide fault indication as well as performance and diagnosis information.

ODI (Open Datalink Interface) – A Novell device driver that is similar to Microsoft's NDIS. ODI is the interface between Netware software and the network interface card.

OID (Object Identifier) – A series of integers separated by periods that denotes the exact path from the root of the MIB tree to a node in the tree.

OSI (Open Systems Interconnection) – A seven-layer communications architecture model developed by the ISO for the interconnection of data communication systems.

Packet Switching – A data-switching technique in which information to be transmitted is organized in "packets." Packets have a format that includes different fields such as the source address field, the destination address field, and the information field. The source address and destination address are located in the packet's header. The destination address enables a packet to be forwarded from one switch in the network to another until it reaches its destination.

Payload – The part of an ATM cell that contains the actual information being transferred, as opposed to the cell header. The payload occupies 48 octets.

PBX (Private Branch Exchange) – A private switching system that serves an organization, such as a business. The PBX is usually located on the organization's premises.

PCI (Protocol Control Information) – Information exchanged by peer entities at different sites on the network to instruct the receiving peer entity to perform a service function. The PCI is called by the names header and trailer.

PCR (Peak Cell Rate) – The maximum rate (in cells per second) that an end system can transmit.

PDU (Protocol Data Unit) – A term used to describe the data unit that is sent to a lower layer protocol entity by the layer above. The PDU consists of the service data unit and the protocol control information (header and/or trailer appended at the layer generating the PDU). PDU = SDU + PCI.

PMD (Physical Medium Dependent) – A sublayer in the Physical layer that provides bit timing and performs the actual transmission of bits over the physical medium.

PNNI (Private Network-Network Interface) – An ATM Forum NNI specified for private networks.

PRI (Primary Rate Interface) – An ISDN specification that provides 23 64-kbps bearer channels (or B-channels) and one 64-kbps data channel (or D-channel). It is also known as the 23B + D service.

Proxy Agent – An SNMP agent that can communicate with and/or monitor a non-SNMP device and return management information to an SNMP manager.

PTI (Payload Type Identifier) – An encoding in the payload type field of the cell header that describes the AAL and EFCI status.

PVC (Permanent Virtual Circuit) – A connection between a given source-destination pair that is established via the network management system to be used for a long period.

QoS (Quality of Service) – A term used to describe a set of performance parameters that characterize the traffic over a given VC.

RARP (Reverse ARP) – A protocol defined in RFC 903 to enable a diskless workstation to discover its own IP address.

Registration – A mechanism by which a client, such as an LEC or MPC, provides address information to the appropriate server (e.g., LES in LANE and route server in MPOA).

RFC (Request for Comment) – IETF documents that contain proposed standards and specifications.

RM (Resource Management) – The management of the actual resources in an ATM network. It includes buffer allocation and bandwidth management through virtual path (VP) provisioning.

RM Cell (Resource Management Cell) – A special control cell used to convey information on bandwidth availability, congestion, and impending congestion to the source.

RS (Route Server) – A physical device that runs one or more network layer routing protocols and provides network layer routing forwarding descriptions to MPOA clients in an MPOA system.

RSVP (Resource Reservation Protocol) – A protocol developed to support different QoS classes in the Internet.

SAAL (Signaling AAL) – The AAL for the control plane. The SAAL provides reliable transport of Q.2931 (signaling) messages between Q.2931 entities over the ATM layer.

SAP (Service Access Point) – The point at which the services of an OSI layer are made available to the next higher layer. The SAP is named according to the layer providing the service. For example, Transport services are provided to the Session layer at a Transport SAP (TSAP), and Network services are provided to the Transport layer at a Network SAP (NSAP).

SAR (Segmentation and Reassembly) – The lower half of the AAL that converts the PDUs received from the convergence sublayer into cells at the source, and reassembles the cell payloads received from the ATM layer at the destination.

SCR (Sustainable Cell Rate) – A parameter that specifies the average rate at which a bursty source can send traffic over a given VC.

SDU (Service Data Unit) – A term used to describe the data unit received from the next high layer protocol entity. The SDU is a component part of the PDU.

SEAL (Simple and Efficient Adaptation Layer) – The original name for AAL type 5.

Signaling – The exchange of messages in a network to inform the user what actions to take in order to set up, maintain, and terminate a call.

SNMP (Simple Network Management Protocol) – An IETF-defined network management protocol for monitoring and controlling network devices in IP networks. SNMPv1 is documented in RFC 1157 and SNMPv2 is documented in RFC 1448.

SNMP Agent – Software in a network device that is responsible for handling SNMP requests and generating traps.

SNMP Manager – Software in a network management station that is responsible for generating SNMP queries and commands that are destined for SNMP agents. The SNMP manager is also responsible for analyzing SNMP responses and traps received from SNMP agents.

SPTS (Single Program Transport Stream) – An MPEG-2 transport stream that consists of only one program.

SS7 Network – A packet-switched, out-of-band signaling network for transporting circuit-related information between exchanges for call setup and call release.

SSCF (Service-Specific Coordination Function) – Part of the service-specific convergence sublayer (SSCS) that provides a service-independent adaptation of user data to the service specific connection-oriented protocol (SSCOP).

SSCOP (Service-Specific Connection-Oriented Protocol) – Part of the SSCS that provides error control and guaranteed data delivery integrity.

SSCS (Service-Specific Convergence Sublayer) – A component of the convergence sublayer of the AAL that is dependent on the traffic class to be converted.

Statistical Multiplexing (Stat Mux) – A version of TDM in which no slot is dedicated to any user. Time slots are allocated on a dynamic basis only to active users.

SVC (Switched Virtual Circuit) – A connection that is dynamically established and torn down via signaling.

T-*n* Carrier – Standard North American digital transmission technique for sending information at DS-*n* rates. T-1 (or T1) is used for transmitting at the DS-1 rate (1.544 Mbps), and T-3 (or T3) is used for transmitting at the DS3 rate (44.768 Mbps or 28 T1 streams).

TA (Terminal Adapter) – A functional group, defined for N-ISDN, that enables non-ISDN equipment (e.g., TE2 devices) to communicate with the ISDN network.

TCP (Transmission Control Protocol) – A transport protocol that provides reliable transmission of data in IP-based networks. TCP is documented in RFC 793.

TDM (Time-Division Multiplexing) – See **Multiplexing**.

TE1 (Terminal Equipment Type 1) – A functional group, defined for N-ISDN, that provides ISDN-specific functions. TE1 devices are N-ISDN compatible terminals.

TE2 (Terminal Equipment Type 2) – A functional group, defined for N-ISDN, that provides non-ISDN-specific functions. A TE2 device is a non-ISDN compatible device. An example of a TE2 device is the analog telephone.

TMN (Telecommunications Management Network) – An ITU-T standard for managing a public switched telecommunication network.

Traffic Contract – An agreement between a user and the network regarding the expected QoS to be provided by the network and the set of traffic parameters that the user is expected to comply with.

Traffic Shaping – A method of altering the characteristics of the traffic entering the ATM network by buffering the data temporarily and sending the cells at a rate that conforms with the traffic contract. The goal is to reduce the PCR, limit the burst length, or reduce the cell delay variation.

Trailer – Protocol control information located at the end of a PDU.

Trap – An unsolicited message sent by an SNMP agent to a network management station to alert the latter of a specific network event.

TS (Transport Stream) – A stream provided by the MPEG-2 system layer that consists of 188-byte packets which can contain multiple programs.

UBR (Unspecified Bit Rate) – A best-effort ATM traffic type with no quality of service guarantees.

UDP (User Datagram Protocol) – A connectionless transport protocol used in IP networks and documented in RFC 768.

UNI (User-Network Interface) – The interface point between ATM end users and a private ATM switch, or between a private ATM switch and the public carrier ATM network. UNI also refers to the standards adopted by the ATM Forum to define the connections between users or end systems and a local switch.

Unicast – A transmission destined for a single user in a network.

UPC (Usage Parameter Control) – The set of actions taken by the network to monitor and control user traffic in order to ensure that a user conforms to the contract established between him/her and the network.

VBR (Variable Bit Rate) – A service category defined by the ATM Forum that supports data traffic with variable bit rate, peak, and average traffic parameters.

VC (Virtual Channel) – A communication channel that provides for the sequential unidirectional transport of ATM cells.

VCC (Virtual Channel Connection) – A concatenation of virtual channel links that extends between the points where the ATM service users access the ATM layer.

VCI (Virtual Channel Identifier) – A 16-bit number that uniquely identifies a VC within a VP.

VCL (Virtual Channel Link) – A means of unidirectional transport of ATM cells between the point where a VCI value is assigned and the point where that value is translated or removed.

VC Switch (Virtual Channel Switch) – An ATM switch that terminates VPCs and translates VCI values.

Virtual Scheduling – A method used to determine the conformance of an arriving cell. Virtual Scheduling works by comparing a "theoretical arrival time" of a cell to the actual arrival time. If the actual arrival time is less than the theoretical arrival time by more than a predefined value, the cell is classified as non-conforming; otherwise, it is conforming.

VLAN (Virtual LAN) – A logical grouping of users in a switched network that reduces the overhead associated with adds, moves, and changes in a network. Information transmitted by one member of a VLAN is received by all members of the VLAN. Thus, a VLAN is a broadcast domain defined over a switched network.

VoD (Video-on-Demand) – A technology that permits a user to remotely select and play a video tape via a communication network.

VP (Virtual Path) – A set of VCs grouped together between switches.

VPC (Virtual Path Connection) – A concatenation of VP links between a source switch and the point where the VCs in a VP are unbundled.

VPI (Virtual Path Identifier) – An 8-bit value in a UNI cell header or a 12-bit value in an NNI cell header that provides a unique identity for a group of VCs.

VPL (Virtual Path Link) – A means of unidirectional transport of ATM cells between the point where a VPI value is assigned and the point where that value is translated or removed.

VP Switch (Virtual Path Switch) – An ATM switch that terminates VPCs and translates VPI values but not VCI values.

WAN (Wide Area Network) – A network, such as the public telephone network, that spans a large geographical area.

REFERENCES

[1]   E.B. Carne, *Telecommunications Primer: Signals, Building Blocks, and Networks,* IEEE Press/Prentice Hall, Inc., 1995.

[2]   ISO International Standard 7498, *Information Processing Systems – Open Systems Interconnection – Basic Reference Model,* 1983.

[3]   ITU-T Recommendation X.21, *Interface between Data Terminal Equipment and Data Circuit-Terminating Equipment for Synchronous Operation on Public Data Networks,* 1992.

[4]   ISO International Standard 4335, *Data Communication – High Level Data Link Control – Elements of Procedures,* 1979.

[5]   *Synchronous Data Link Control Concepts,* IBM Publication GA27-3093-3, 4th edition, 1986.

[6]   J.B. Postel, "Interconnection Protocol Approaches," *IEEE Transactions on Communications,* Volume COM-28, 1980, pp. 604–611.

[7]   ITU-T Recommendation X.400, *Message Handling Systems: System Model Service Elements,* 1993.

[8]   ITU-T Recommendation X.500, *The Directory: Overview of Concepts, Models and Service,* 1993.

[9]   ITU-T Recommendation X.25, *Interface between Data Terminal Equipment (DTE) and Data Circuit-Terminating Equipment (DCE) for Packet Mode and Connected to Public Data Networks by Dedicated Circuit,* 1993.

[10] ITU-T Recommendation Q.700, *Introduction to ITU-T Signaling System No. 7,* 1993.

[11]   ITU-T Recommendation I.411, *ISDN User-Network Interfaces – Reference Configurations*, 1993.

[12]   ATM Forum, *Introducing the ATM Forum*, http://www.atmforum.com/atmforum/atm_introduction.html.

[13]   ATM Forum, *ATM User-Network Interface (UNI) Signaling Specification Version 4.0*, af-sig-0061.000, 1996.

[14]   ITU-T Recommendation X.213, *Information Technology – Network Service Definition for Open Systems Interconnection*, 1992.

[15]   ISO 6523, *Data Interchange – Structures for the Identification of Organization*, 1984.

[16]   ISO 3166, *Codes for the Representation of Names of Countries*, 1988.

[17]   ITU-T Recommendation E.164, *Numbering Plan for the ISDN Era*, 1991.

[18]   "U.S. Government Open Systems Interconnection Profile," U.S. Federal Information Processing Standards Publication 146, April 1988.

[19]   ITU-T Recommendation Q.2931, *Broadband Integrated Services Digital Networks (B-ISDN) – Digital Subscriber Signalling No. 2 (DSS 2) – User Network Interface Layer 3 Specification for Basic Call/Connection Control*, 1995.

[20]   ITU-T Recommendation Q.2110, *B-ISDN ATM Adaptation Layer – Service Specific Connection Oriented Protocol (SSCOP)*, 1995.

[21]   ATM Forum, *ATM User-Network Interface Specification Version 3.1*, 1994.

[22]   ATM Forum, *ATM User-Network Interface Specification Version 3.0*, 1993.

[23]   ITU-T Draft Recommendation Q.93B, *B-ISDN User-Network Interface Layer 3 Specification for Basic Call/Bearer Control*, 1993.

[24]   ATM Forum, *Traffic Management Specification Version 4.0*, af-tm-0056-000, 1996.

[25]   ATM Forum, "ATM Service Categories: The Benefit to the User," http://www.atmforum.com/atmforum/library/service_categories.html, 1996.

[26]   ITU-T Recommendation I.363, *B-ISDN ATM Adaptation Layer (AAL) Specification*, 1993.

[27]   ITU-T Recommendation M.3400, *TMN Management Functions*, 1992.

[28]   RFC 1157, "A Simple Network Management Protocol (SNMP)," D. Case *et al.*, eds., May 1990.

[29] ISO/IEC 9596-1, *Information Technology – Open Systems Interconnection – Common Management Information Protocol, Part 1: Specification*, 1991.

[30] ITU-T Recommendation M.3010, *Principles for a Telecommunications Management Network (TMN)*, 1991.

[31] ITU-T Recommendation I.610, *B-ISDN Operation and Maintenance Principles and Functions*, 1993.

[32] ATM Forum, *Customer Network Management (CNM) for ATM Public Network Service (M3 Specification)*, af-nm-0019-000, 1994.

[33] ATM Forum, *M4 Interface Requirements and Logical MIB*, af-nm-0020-000, 1994.

[34] ATM Forum, *M4 Network-View Interface Requirements and Logical MIB*, af-nm-0058-000, 1996.

[35] RFC 1695, "Definitions of Managed Objects for ATM Management Version 8 using SMIv2," M. Ahmed and K. Tesink, eds., August 1994.

[36] ATM Forum, *CMIP Specification for the M4 Interface*, af-nm-0027-000, 1995.

[37] ITU-T Recommendation I.326, *Functional Architecture of Transport Network Based on ATM*, 1995.

[38] ATM Forum, *Integrated Local Management Interface (ILMI) Specification Version 4.0*, af-ilmi-0065-000, 1996.

[39] ITU-T Recommendation I.361, *B-ISDN ATM Layer Specification*, 1993.

[40] Internet Draft "Definitions of Supplemental Managed Objects for ATM Management," F. Ly, M. Noto and K. Tesink, editors, draft-ietf-atommib-atm2-08.txt, December 1996.

[41] A. Leinwand and K.F. Conroy, *Network Management: A Practical Perspective*, 2nd edition, Addison-Wesley Publishing Co., 1996.

[42] W. Stallings, *SNMP, SNMPv2, and CMIP: The Practical Guide to Network-Management Standards*, Addison-Wesley Publishing Co., 1993.

[43] U. Black, *Network Management Standards: SNMP, CMIP, TMN, MIBs and Object Libraries*, 2nd edition, McGraw-Hill, 1995.

[44] ATM Forum, *Traffic Management Specification Version 4.0*, af-tm-0056.000, 1996.

[45] G. Niestegge, "The 'Leaky Bucket' Policing Method in the ATM (Asynchronous Transfer Mode) Network," *International Journal of Digital and Analog Communication Systems*, Volume 3, 1990, pp. 187–197.

[46]   M.G. Hluchyj and N. Yin, "On the Queueing Behavior of Multiplexed Leaky Bucket Regulated Sources," *Proceedings of the IEEE INFOCOM'93*, San Francisco, March 30–April 1, 1993, pp. 672–679.

[47]   F. Bonomi and K.W. Fendick, "The Rate-Based Flow Control Framework for the Available Bit Rate ATM Service," *IEEE Networks*, Volume 9, Number 2, March/April 1995, pp. 25–39.

[48]   H.T. Kung and R. Morris, "Credit-Based Flow Control for ATM Networks," *IEEE Networks*, Volume 9, Number 2, March/April 1995, pp. 40–48.

[49]   J.F. Mollenauer, "New Prospects for ATM Flow Control," *Business Communications Review*, March 1997, pp. 46–50.

[50]   K.K. Ramakrishnan and P. Newman, "ATM Flow Control: Inside the Great Debate," *Data Communications*, June 1995, pp. 111–120.

[51]   "Quantum Flow Control Version 2.0," FCC-SPEC-95-1, http://www.qfc.org, July 1995.

[52]   ATM Forum, *Interim Inter-switch Signaling Protocol (IISP) Specification v1.0*, af-pnni-0026.000, 1994.

[53]   ATM Forum, *Private Network-Network Interface Specification Version 1.0 (PNNI 1.0)*, af-pnni-0066.000, 1996.

[54]   ATM Forum, *LAN Emulation Over ATM Version 1.0*, af-lane-0021.000, 1995.

[55]   RFC 1483, "Multiprotocol Encapsulation Over ATM Adaptation Layer 5," J. Heinanen, ed., 1993.

[56]   RFC 1932, "IP Over ATM: A Framework Document," R. Cole, D. Shur, and C. Villamizar, eds., 1996.

[57]   RFC 1577, "Classical IP and ARP Over ATM," M. Laubach, ed., 1994.

[58]   RFC 1293, "Inverse Address Resolution Protocol," T. Bradley and C. Brown, eds., 1992.

[59]   G. Armitage, "Support for Multicast Over UNI 3.0/3.1 based ATM Networks," Internet-Draft draft-ietf-ipm-ipmc-12.txt, 1996.

[60]   J.V. Luciani, D. Katz, D. Piscitello, and B. Cole, "NBMA Next Hop Resolution Protocol (NHRP)," Internet-Draft draft-ietf-rolc-nhrp-09.txt, 1996.

[61]   RFC 1633, "Integrated Services in the Internet Architecture: an Overview," R. Braden, D. Clark, and S. Shenker eds., 1994.

[62]   J. Wroclawski, "The Use of RSVP with IETF Integrated Services," Internet-Draft draft-ietf-intserv-rsvp-use-00.txt, 1996.

[63]   R. Braden, L. Zhang, S. Berson, S. Herzog, and S. Jamin, "Resource ReSerVation Protocol (RSVP) Version 1 Functional Specification," Internet-Draft draft-ietf-rsvp-spec-10, 1996.

[64]   S. Shenker and C. Patridge, "Specification of Guaranteed Quality of Service," Internet-Draft draft-ietf-intserv-guaranteed-svc-02.txt, 1995.

[65]   S. Shenker, C. Patridge, and J. Wroclawski, "Specification of Controlled Delay Quality of Service," Internet-Draft draft-ietf-intserv-controlled-del-svc-02.txt, 1995.

[66]   S. Shenker, C. Patridge, B. Davie, and L. Breslau, "Specification of Predictive Quality of Service," Internet-Draft draft-ietf-intserv-predictive-svc-01.txt, 1995.

[67]   J. Wroclawski, "Specification of Controlled-Load Network Element Service," Internet-Draft draft-ietf-intserv-ctrl-load-svc-01.txt, 1995.

[68]   RFC 1821, "Integration of Real-time Services in an IP-ATM Network Architecture," M. Borden, E. Crawley, B. Davie, and S. Batsell, eds., 1995.

[69]   R.O. Onvural and V. Srinivasan, "A Framework for Supporting RSVP Flows over ATM Networks," Internet-Draft draft-onvural-srinivasa-rsvp-atm-00.txt, 1996.

[70]   L. Berger, "RSVP Over ATM: Framework and UNI 3.0/3.1 Method," Internet-Draft draft-berger-rsvp-over-atm-00.txt, 1996.

[71]   ATM Forum, *Multi-Protocol Over ATM Version 1,* af-mpoa-0087.000, 1977.

[72]   Ipsilon Networks, "IP Switching: The Intelligence of Routing, the Performance of Switching," http://www.ipsilon.com/productinfo/techwp1.html, 1996.

[73]   P. Newman, T. Lyon, and G. Minshall, "Flow Labelled IP: Connectionless ATM Under IP," Network+Interop, Las Vegas, April 1996.

[74]   RFC 1987, "Ipsilon's General Switch Management Protocol Specification," P. Newman *et al.,* eds., 1996.

[75]   RFC 1953, "Ipsilon Flow Management Protocol Specification for IPv4," P. Newman *et al.,* eds., 1996.

[76]   E. Roberts, "IP on Speed," *Data Communications,* March 1997, pp. 84–96.

[77]   ITU-T Recommendation I-122, *Framework for Providing Additional Packet Mode Bearer Service,* 1988.

[78]   ITU-T Recommendation I-233, *Frame Relaying Bearer Service,* 1991.

[79]   ATM Forum, *Frame-Based User-Network Interface (FUNI) Specifications*, af-saa-0031-00, 1995.

[80]   ATM Forum, *ATM Data Exchange Interface (DXI) Specification Version 1.0*, af-dxi-0014-00, 1993.

[81]   ITU-T Recommendation Q.922, *ISDN Data Link Layer Specification for Frame Mode Bearer Services*, 1992.

[82]   RFC 1490, "Multiprotocol Interconnect Over Frame Relay," T. Bradley, C. Brown, and A. Malis, eds., 1993.

[83]   ITU-T Recommendation I.555, *Frame Relaying Bearer Service Interworking*, 1993.

[84]   Frame Relay Forum, *Frame Relay/ATM PVC Network Interworking Agreement*, FRF.5, 1994.

[85]   Frame Relay Forum, *Frame Relay/ATM PVC Service Interworking Agreement*, FRF.8, 1994.

[86]   U. Black, *Frame Relay Networks: Specifications and Implementations*, 2nd edition, McGraw-Hill, Inc., 1996.

[87]   Digital Audio-Visual Council, *DAVIC 1.0 Specification*, Revision 3.1, 1996.

[88]   ATM Forum, *Audiovisual Multimedia Services: Video on Demand Specification 1.0*, af-saa-0049-000, 1995.

[89]   ITU-T Recommendation H.222.0, *Information Technology – Generic Coding for Moving Pictures and Associated Audio – Part 1: Systems*, 1995.

[90]   ITU-T Recommendation Q.2130, *B-ISDN Signaling ATM Adaptation Layer – Service-Specific Co-ordination Function for Support of Signaling at the User to Network Interface (SSCF at UNI)*, 1995.

[91]   ITU-T Recommendation H.222.1, *Multimedia Multiplex and Synchronization for Audiovisual Communication in ATM Environments*, 1995.

[92]   ISO/IEC DIS 13818-6, *Information Technology – Generic Coding for Moving Pictures and Associated Audio – Part 6: MPEG-2 Digital Storage Media – Command and Control (DSM-CC)*, 1995.

[93]   ITU-T Recommendation H.245, *Line Transmission of Non-Telephone Signals – Control Protocol for Multimedia Communication*, 1995.

[94]   ATM Forum, *Circuit Emulation Service Interoperability Specification*, AF-SAA-0032.000, September 1995.

[95] ATM Forum, "Circuit Emulation Service Interoperability Specification Version 2.0," Baseline Draft 95-1504R2, June 1996.

[96] AT&T, *Telecommunications Transmission Engineering Volume 1: Principles,* 2nd edition, 1977.

[97] ATM Forum, *Voice and Telephony Over ATM – ATM Trunking Using AAL1 for Narrowband Services, Version 1.0,* af-vtoa-0089.000, 1997.

[98] K.D. Kovarik and P. Maveddat, "Multi-Rate ISDN," *IEEE Communications Magazine,* April 1994, pp. 48–54.

[99] Bellcore, "Generic Requirements for the Switched DS1/Switched Fractional DS1 Capability from an ISDN Interface (SWF-DS1/ISDN)," TR-NWT-001203, Issue 2, December 1992.

[100] J. Duncanson, "Inverse Multiplexing," *IEEE Communications Magazine,* April 1994, pp. 34–41.

[101] P.H. Fredette, "The Past, Present, and Future of Inverse Multiplexing," *IEEE Communications Magazine,* April 1994, pp. 42–46.

[102] ATM Forum, *Inverse Multiplexing for ATM (IMA) Specification, Version 1.0,* af-phy-0086.000, 1997.

[103] ADSL Forum, "General Introduction to Copper Access Technologies," http://www.adsl.com/adsl/general_tutorial.html

INDEX